Do You **Still** Believe in Miracles?

Do You **Still** Believe in Miracles?

*An Apologetic Exposé by a Liberal,
Bible-Believing, Evangelical Pastor*

JOHN RUIZ

WIPF & STOCK · Eugene, Oregon

DO YOU STILL BELIEVE IN MIRACLES?
An Apologetic Exposé by a Liberal, Bible-Believing, Evangelical Pastor

Copyright © 2025 John Ruiz. All rights reserved. Except for brief quotations in critical publications or reviews, no part of this book may be reproduced in any manner without prior written permission from the publisher. Write: Permissions, Wipf and Stock Publishers, 199 W. 8th Ave., Suite 3, Eugene, OR 97401.

Wipf & Stock
An Imprint of Wipf and Stock Publishers
199 W. 8th Ave., Suite 3
Eugene, OR 97401

www.wipfandstock.com

PAPERBACK ISBN: 979-8-3852-5856-7
HARDCOVER ISBN: 979-8-3852-5857-4
EBOOK ISBN: 979-8-3852-5858-1

09/02/25

Contents

PART ONE

Beginning the Conversation | 3

The Quest for Christ and the Reality of Jesus | 9

Women's Rights and the Bible | 20

Inclusiveness and Universality | 26

Abortion and Truth | 31

Popularity, Comfort, and Blindness | 40

Do No Harm | 46

New Gnosticism and the Canonical Bible | 53

Authority and Freedom | 60

Truth a Foundation for Peace | 65

Trapped in Works and the Rediscovery of Free Grace | 72

PART TWO

The Conversation Continues | 79

Paternalistic Tendencies in Progressive Theology | 82

A Conversation with a United Methodist Bishop | 88

Struggles with Science | 96

Grace and Truth | 102

CONTENTS

Jesus Is Good News | 107

Glimpses of God | 111

Life Is Better with Jesus | 120

Bibliography | 125

PART ONE

Beginning the Conversation

*Each part . . . working properly, promotes the
body's growth in building itself up in love.*

EPHESIANS 4:16B

IF YOU HAVE EXPERIENCED reading a Bible written in your own language, then find a liberal Christian and say, "Thank you!" For there was a time in Christian history when reading a Bible in one's language was an idea espoused by the liberal Christian, and such an idea was too risky within the more conservative or orthodox voices within the Christian "choir."

The purpose of this conversation is not to belittle the liberal Christian. Rather, the purpose is to passionately and powerfully uplift biblical truth, simply the truth of one pastor and the experiences of this Bible-believing, evangelical, liberal pastor who is called to live and serve within a liberal branch of the Christian family. In this way, there are times when this conversation might take on a type of exposé feel, since some of the situations and teachings encountered within a liberal seminary education and within the liberal church are hard to imagine and might seem unbelievable if they were not personally experienced.

Therefore, my intention is for a much-needed wake up call for many faithful persons within liberal veins of Christianity by offering a peek behind the scenes of the inner-workings of the liberal church. In this way, this conversation on a personal level will be added to the developing conservative, orthodox, Bible-believing, confessing movements within my own denomination as we struggle within the church to resuscitate the soul of the denomination. Further, it is my prayer that this honest opening might inspire dialogue within other branches of the Christian family, point out variations in thought that have led away from the living vine of Christ, and finally, urge the liberal voices within the Christian family to rediscover free grace as the foundation for all that we do.

I have been in ministry nearly twenty years, and have served as a United Methodist pastor and as a hospital chaplain in a metropolitan area. My seminary education was at the Methodist Theological School in Ohio from 1993 to 1996. Several mandatory classes that I took during my seminary education were taught by professors who were very proud of their membership in the Jesus Seminar. The Jesus Seminar and the ideas of this group will be discussed in detail in the chapter "The Quest for Christ and the Reality of Jesus."

The United Methodist Church in the United States is part of the liberal voices within the broader Christian family. This may not be the reality within the pews of the local church. However, it is very much the reality within the context of the current United Methodist Discipline and much of the "leadership" of the church. The United Methodist Church and several other liberal denominations that traveled similar paths have slowly drifted away from the core social action/adoration of God union, which is the heart of the movement's gift to the broader Christian community and the world itself.

This social action/adoration of God union has drifted away from free, universal, responsible grace that is the truth of Jesus, which is found in the canonical Gospels and the canonical Bible cherished by so many. Too often, free grace has seemed like cheap grace, as the significance of the cross of Christ has been de-emphasized. Too often, universal grace has developed into a much, much smaller vision of inclusion, which by its very nature means that while including some, others are also now on the outside looking in. Too often, responsible grace has taken on a witness that seems an awful lot like relative grace, where everything goes but nothing really matters, and the meaning and joy found in responsible grace is lost.

One of the realities I have experienced time and time again as a pastor in the local church and as a hospital chaplain is the faithfulness of individuals, the peace that passes understanding, and the faith that hopes beyond reason. Another is the true astonishment and sadness found with many of the local churches that are continuing to lose members. Some of these (usually) smaller churches are closing, and many others, try as they might, are often failing to attract new, younger members into the life of the church.

Later, in the chapter "Inclusiveness and Universality," I will examine some of the staggering membership trends within liberal and conservative/orthodox denominations in the church. Time and time again as a pastor within the local churches I have served, I have heard about methodologies for growing the church. The book *Five Practices of a Faithful Congregation* written by Robert Schnase, a United Methodist bishop serving in the Missouri Conference, is a perfect example of the focus on methodology. Schnase's book offers methods that the local church can perform to attract new persons.[1] Much of the book can be helpful and lead to fruitful work and new programming; however, his book never touches upon the theological reasons for the incredible difficulties found in church growth within liberal church settings. Sooner or later, Christians read their Bibles and then question the official positions of the broader church. And seeing incongruences, these people chose to travel down the road to another church where things seem more open and in line to what they have found within their personal Bible readings; thus leaving the faithful member of the local liberal church ever more saddened.

Further, spontaneous responses of sheer joy are rarely found within larger gatherings and especially within the liberal leadership of the church. In fact, many times spontaneous responses of sheer joy within larger church gatherings are seen with suspicion, as somehow inauthentic or overly emotional.

---

1. Schnase, *Five Practices*.

I believe this occurs because of a drifting away from free grace into a position where individual works are elevated again and again. All this means is faithful people (many times colleagues and personal friends) might be putting in longer and longer hours working within their local church and yet are seeing less and less results from their labor and are experiencing fewer and fewer moments of sheer joy.

My final hope is that a constructive dialogue with liberal voices within Christianity will lead to a new discovery of free grace and a renewed union of social action/adoration of God. This rediscovery, this reformation can allow the liberal veins of the Christian church to return to their first love once again and be the much needed blessing to the world which is part of the liberal church's long, rich, and fruitful history.

PART TWO

This book is a book within a book. The first half of the book was completed in 2008 and is the writing of a Bible believing liberal pastor continuing to process his seminary experience and come to terms with teachings that seemed unusual and even outside the lines of orthodox faith. As a young pastor, I believed that these ideas would be limited to the confines of the seminary and therefore not be found in the leadership of the United Methodist Church.

When I completed the first half of this apologetic, I tried the traditional ways to publish a book including the United Methodist Publishing House, Abingdon Press. The book was turned down.

Today, in the fall of 2024, I am returning to write a follow-up. I am writing this second half because teachings that I had experienced that seemed unusual and even outside the lines of orthodox faith are now prevalent throughout all aspects of the United Methodist Church. They can be found within the Episcopacy, many clergy, and even the local church.

For the past fifty years, the United Methodist Church has been embroiled in a debate concerning homosexuality and the place of homosexuality within the church. As a result, my experience was anytime anyone would try to raise concerns about the theological teachings found within some areas of the church—including the denial of the virgin birth, the bodily resurrection of Jesus, and the Trinity—these arguments would be shut-down and censored. Often, those seeking debate and theological clarification would be labeled as anti-gay, bigoted, and hateful.

On May 1, 2022, the United Methodist Church experienced a schism and a new denomination called the Global Methodist Church was launched. The Global Methodist Church seeks to be a global church that represents a traditional understanding of marriage being one man and one woman, and resides firmly within an orthodox understanding of the Wesleyan tradition. This means the Global Methodist Church affirms the virgin birth, the bodily resurrection of Jesus and the Trinity.

It is my prayer that this apologetic can now be heard within the United Methodist Church and spur debate that concentrates on theological understandings and the ramifications that are predictably lived out when traditional orthodox teaching of the church are jettisoned and denied. This is not to say that the entire United Methodist Church and their doctrine has jettisoned an affirmation of the virgin birth, the bodily resurrection of Jesus, and the Trinity. At the same time, this apologetic demonstrates that it would be dishonest to claim that in some areas of the United Methodist Church, both at a seminary level and (at times) within positions of leadership within the church, there are occasions when the virgin birth, the bodily resurrection of Jesus, and the Trinity have been denied or reinterpreted in a way not conducive to orthodox Christian theology.

It is also my prayer that those in the Christian family who have chosen not to jettison and deny traditional orthodox teachings of the church will be encouraged to continue to boldly proclaim the good news of Jesus Christ to a world in need. For God is faithful and good and remains very active in the lives of the people, within the body of Christ, the Christian church, and within human history.

QUESTIONS FOR REVIEW, REFLECTION, AND DISCUSSION

1. What is the core of the liberal Christian movement and the subsequent gift to the broader Christian community and the world?

2. What is the meaning of grace as understood through Jesus and found in the canonical Gospels (Matthew, Mark, Luke and John) and the books of the New Testament?

3. What is often lost in larger gatherings within the liberal church today and especially within the liberal leadership of the church? What does the author suggest is the reason for this? What are your thoughts?

4. How have discussions concerning theology been consistently shut down by leadership within the United Methodist Church?

The Quest for Christ and the Reality of Jesus

The law indeed was given through Moses: grace and truth came through Jesus Christ.

JOHN 1:17

MY EXPERIENCE OF THE quest for Christ began during my seminary education at the Methodist Theological Seminary in Ohio. I attended seminary from 1993 to 1996. It began with a straw man.

A straw man is a tactic used in debate when one takes the weakest point of another's position and by casting that point as an absurdity dismisses the other without ever engaging their thought. In the political arena, a straw man argument can be very effective and is used all the time. However, in the pursuit of theological discourse it is unnecessary, unhelpful, and it discourages constructive dialogue. The straw man in this case centers on scriptural methodology, how one sees scripture as currently contained in the Bible and then what methods are best for interpretation.

On the one hand, the straw man continues, is the literal interpretation of the Bible, and on the other hand is the historical critical interpretation of the Bible. It is similar to a scientist saying that to continue your scientific studies you must first decide if the earth is round or flat, an either/or decision that seems absurd in the realms of intellectual thought.

In the study of biblical scripture this either/or dynamic is unhelpful. Clearly, there are passages where a literal interpretation of a passage is appropriate. Luke 18:16 states, "Jesus called them, and said, 'Let the little children come to me, and do not stop them; for it is to such as these that the kingdom of God belongs.'"

At other times a symbolic or dynamic conversational approach is most helpful in the interpretation of a passage. Matt 7:24–27 reads,

> Everyone then who hears these words of mine and acts on them will be like a wise man who built his house upon rock. The rain fell, and the floods came, and the winds blew and beat on the house, but it did not fall because it had been founded on rock. And everyone who hears these words of mine and does not act on them will be like a foolish man, who built his house upon sand. The rain fell, and the floods came, and the winds blew and beat upon the house, and it fell- and great was its fall!

Obviously, this instruction is meant for spiritual thought and is not meant to be read as a manual for architects. Pope Benedict XVI discusses the benefits and limitations of the historical-critical method when he writes,

> The historical-critical method is an indispensable tool, given the structure of Christian faith. But we need to add two points. This method is a fundamental dimension of exegesis, but it does not exhaust the interpretive task for someone who sees Biblical writings as a single corpus of Scripture inspired by God.[1]

Benedict continues,

> The second point is to recognize the limits of the historical-critical method itself. For someone who considers himself directly addressed by the Bible today, the method's first limit is that by its very nature is has to leave the Biblical world in the past. It is a *historical* method, and that means that it investigates the then-current context of events in which the texts originated. It attempts to

---

1. Benedict, *Jesus of Nazareth*, xvi.

> identify and to understand the past-as it was in itself-with the greatest possible precision,
> In order to find out what the author could have said and intended to say in the context and mentality and events of the time. To the extent that it remains true to itself, the historical method not only has to investigates the Biblical word as a thing of the past, but also has to let it remain in the past. It can glimpse points of contact with the present and can try and apply the Biblical word to the present; the one thing it cannot do is make it into something present *today*-that would be overstepping its bounds. Its very precision in interpreting reality of the past is both its strength and its limits.[2]

The quest for Christ movement was very strong in some of the required classes that I took during my seminary years. I remember a class on Christology where we had four required books. Early in the class the professor informed us that he did not find the "Trinity to be very convincing," therefore we would not be learning about the Holy Trinity.

One of the required books in this mandatory class for persons seeking a Master's degree in Divinity and hoping to serve in the local church was *Models of God: Theology for an Ecological, Nuclear Age* written by Sallie McFague. The purpose of the book can be summarized with the following quote:

> If theologians and students of religion are to be a part of the solution to the problem posed by the unprecedented nuclear knowledge that human beings now possess, they must, I believe, answer the call to deconstruct and reconstruct the traditional symbols of Christian faith. This task suggests that Christian theology, in our time at least, cannot be merely or mainly hermeneutics, that is interpretation of the tradition, a translation of ancient creeds and concepts to make them relevant for contemporary culture. Rather, theology must be self-consciously constructive, willing to think differently than in the past. If one reflects on the contrast between the theologies of Paul, Augustine, Luther, Schleiermacher, and Barth (just

---

2. Benedict, *Jesus of Nazareth*, xvi.

to take a sampling of the tradition) as to their basic images, root metaphors, concepts, and assumptions about reality one has to acknowledge an enormous variety, all of it however, capable of being accommodated with the Christian paradigm. Theology in our day needs to be self-consciously constructive in order to free itself from traditional notions of divine sovereignty sufficiently to be able to experiment with other and more appropriate metaphors and models that may help us cope with the "question now before the human species . . . whether life or death will prevail on earth."[3]

It was not long before it became clear that those professors who followed or espoused the teachings of the Jesus Seminar basically thought the canonical Gospels found in the Bible (Matthew, Mark, Luke and John) got it wrong or were created by man (not divinely inspired) and were now in need of new images or models of Jesus. This occurred without ever addressing what is distinctive within the canonical Gospels concerning Jesus, namely the witness that Jesus lived, died on a cross, and rose from the grave, and that grace as understood in and through Jesus and the witness of the canonical Gospels is free, universal, and responsible.

In my "Introduction to the Bible" class in seminary, which was another required class taught by a Jesus Seminar professor, we had an assignment to write a paper on Mark 5:21–43. This is a passage that contains a story. The passage starts with a leader of the synagogue named Jairus weeping at Jesus's feet and asking that Jesus help heal his little daughter. As Jesus and Jairus are on their way to Jairus's home, Jesus is touched by a woman who had been hemorrhaging for twelve years. A dialogue continues and concludes with Jesus healing the woman and saying, "Daughter your faith has made you well; go in peace, and be healed of your disease." The passage then returns to Jairus and his daughter and the healing of the daughter.

A required book within the class as we prepared our papers on this passage was *Mark's Story of Jesus*, written by Werner H.

3. McFague, *Models of God*, 21.

Kebler. I can remember even as a student how surprised I was that we were reading this book that had no bibliography! However, it was a required text, so what is a student to do but fulfill the requirement?

Towards the end of this ninety-six page book, Kebler declares the purpose of his book and his interpretation of the Gospel of Mark. Kebler argues that within the Gospel of Mark, there is a "relentless narrative drive to undermine the authority of the disciples, and especially Peter and the Twelve."[4]

Earlier Kebler clearly stated his argument.

> The nature of Jesus and the purpose of his journey is revealed in view of his death. According to Mark the essence of Jesus can only be revealed in view of his death. For this reason the disciples never came to recognize Jesus, the crucified King, Son of God. They abandoned him at the outset of his last and crucial journey into Jerusalem. And so it is once again left to the enemy—paradoxically, to the man in charge of the execution—to make the Confession the disciples should have made but could not make.[5]

Finally, Kebler writes,

> In his last instructions to the Twelve Jesus proclaims Galilee as the final destination. Then he suffers death on the cross and is enthroned King through death. With death behind him and his kingship assured, he signals the way to Galilee, the new community of the Kingdom of God. The disciples on the other hand act in accordance with the vision of the Kingdom in power. Far from experiencing a change in heart they betray, contradict, deny, and then in the end abandon the suffering dying Jesus. But they have abandoned Jesus on the threshold of his passion, they miss the most important event of the journey into the Kingdom: his enthronement on the cross. The centurion, not the disciples, witness and confess Jesus as Son of God. Unable to grasp the nature of the Kingdom

---

4. Kebler, *Mark's Story of Jesus*, 88.
5. Kebler, *Mark's Story of Jesus*, 83.

and unable to come to terms with the concept of the person of the crucified King, they have now missed their royal enthronement. There is no way the disciples become the leaders of the Kingdom of God.

After the disappearance of the disciples the women, acting in the place of the disciples, bring the disciples' tragedy to its logical conclusion. They fail to convey to the disciples the message of Jesus' resurrection and his return to Galilee. As a result of their failure the disciples never return to Galilee. The Kingdom community of Galilee will not be represented by the disciples.[6]

It might be hard to believe, but in my seminary education I could have graduated without any formal training on any of the canonical Gospels! We were required to take four Bible classes during our seminary education: introduction to the Hebrew Bible, introduction to the New Testament, one upper level Hebrew Bible class and one upper level New Testament class. (I chose a class on Micah for my Hebrew Bible class and a class on Romans for my New Testament class.)

As an aside, at this point, I am sure many are wondering why I would stay at this type of seminary. For me, the answer was easy. I was called to be a pastor while worshiping in the United Methodist Church; therefore, I believed I was supposed to serve in the United Methodist Church. Second, there was so much about the denomination that I loved and continue to love! The empowerment of the laity! The priesthood of all believers! Permission and *encouragement* to read the Bible for myself and to put my faith into action as a Sunday School teacher and Youth Group volunteer. Also, unique to the United Methodism is the concept of an open pulpit and open table.

I love this aspect of the Methodist movement. The open pulpit gives the pastor freedom to preach what they believe God is prodding them to preach in the context of their ministry and their encounter with God's word. The open table was unique to John Wesley's preaching because he believed the church of his day

---

6. Kebler, *Mark's Story of Jesus*, 87.

needed to go to where the people were instead of building a beautiful church and then waiting for the people to come.

In this way, Wesley began open air preaching to people who had very little to no experience with the Christian faith. In many cases, most would not have been baptized. In this context, Wesley's idea of an open table to represent God's free grace would be both bold and appropriate. In other words, all persons gathered, regardless of church experience or any other past life experiences, would be welcome to the table of Christ if they truly believed and felt prodded by God's living spirit. The open table is a characteristic that the United Methodist Church continues today.

Further, the Methodist Theological School in Ohio was part of a consortium where we had to take a class off campus at either the Josephinum Pontifical College or Trinity Lutheran Seminary. Both are a short drive from the Methodist Theological School in Ohio, and I decided to use my elective courses to try and fill in what I saw as major gaps within my training to be an effective pastor. At the Josephinum Pontifical College, I took three Bible classes: one on the Synoptic Gospels (Matthew, Mark and Luke), a class on Johannine literature, and finally a class on wisdom literature in the Bible. At Trinity Lutheran Seminary, I took a class on evangelism.

It was clear that a person would get lower grades in certain classes at the Methodist Theological School in Ohio if they chose to disagree with the teaching of certain professors, but in the larger picture, I figured what was really the big deal of a B-, C or D+ in the grand scheme of things? Also, I must admit that a couple of classes—like the class on Romans taught by Robert Tannehill or the classes taught by Paul Chilcote—were truly amazing and life changing. Further, I believed I could continue to pursue more conventional Christian ideas and truths on my own and not be satisfied with the present curriculum.

In this light, I now turn to two critiques of the quest for Christ movement. The first is the notion that the canonical Gospels basically get the story of Christ and his divinity wrong, and we are left with a myth or a creation of a historical Jesus. I turn to Lee Strobel's book *The Case for Christ* and a conversation he had

Do You Still Believe in Miracles?

with Edwin M. Yamauchi, PhD, a teacher at Miami University in Oxford, Ohio, and a scholar on corroborating evidence concerning Jesus. He was examining if there is "credible evidence for Jesus outside of his biographies."[7]

A summary of Yamauchi's research is astounding! Strobel asked the question, "You've spent forty years studying ancient history and archaeology. What has been the result in your spiritual life? Have your studies bolstered or weakened your faith in Jesus Christ?" Yamauchi responded,

> There is no question—my studies have greatly strengthened and enriched my spiritual life. They have given me a better understanding of the culture and historical context of events. This does not mean that I don't recognize that there are some issues that remain; within this lifetime, we will not have full knowledge.
>
> But these issues don't even begin to undermine my faith in the essential trustworthiness of the gospels and the rest of the New Testament. I think the alternative explanations, which try to account for the spread of Christianity through sociological or psychological reasons, are very, very weak. For me, the historical evidence has reinforced any commitment to Jesus Christ as the Son of God who loves us and died for us and was raised from the dead. It is that simple.[8]

Earlier in the interview Yamauchi related, "The fact is that we have a better historical documentation of Jesus than the founder of any other ancient religion."[9]

Later Strobel asked the question,

> Let's pretend we don't have any of the New Testament or other Christian writings. Even without them, what would we be able to conclude about Jesus from ancient non-Christian sources, such as Josephus, the Talmud, Pliny the younger and others?

---

7. Strobel, *Case for Christ*, 73–91.
8. Strobel, *Case for Christ*, 90.
9. Strobel, *Case for Christ*, 90.

Yamauchi responded, "We would still have a considerable amount of important historical evidence; in fact, it would provide a kind of outline of the life of Jesus. We would know first, Jesus was a Jewish teacher; second, many people believed that he performed miracles and exorcisms; third, some believed he was the Messiah; fourth, he was rejected by Jewish leaders; fifth, he was crucified under Pontius Pilate in the reign of Tiberias; sixth, despite this shameful death, his followers, who believed that he was still alive, spread beyond Palestine so that there were multitudes of them in Rome by A.D. 64; and countryside-men and women, slave and free-worshipped him as God."[10]

Finally, for a brief critique of the Jesus Seminar and the quest for Jesus scholarship found in the conclusions of the Jesus Seminar, I turn to Luke Timothy Johnson and the book *The Real Jesus: The Misguided Quest for the Historical Jesus and the Truth of the Traditional Gospels*. Johnson simply puts into perspective the scholarship of the Jesus Seminar and many church leaders who frequently follow their teaching. Johnson writes,

> The Jesus Seminar is not affiliated with either the Society of Biblical literature or the International Association of new testament scholars, the Studiorum Novi Testamenti Societas. It does not, therefore, represent anything like a consensus view of scholars working in the New Testament, but only the view of a group that has been—for all protestations of diversity—self-selected on the basis of a prior agreement concerning the appropriate goals and methods of studying the gospels and the figure of Jesus. It is from beginning to end, an entrepreneurial venture guided by Robert Funk.
>
> These observations do not detract from the legitimacy of the Seminar or its right to conduct its business as it chooses. But in light of its own statements and media coverage, it is appropriate to clarify its precise academic standing. Sometimes, for example, the phrase "some

---

10. Strobel, *Case for Christ*, 87.

two hundred scholars" has occurred. To someone unacquainted with the immensity and complexity of higher education in America, two hundred scholars may seem an impressive number. In fact, however, it is a very small number when placed against the number of scholars alone who are involved in the work of the SBL (at least half of the 6900 members of the organization), let alone thousands more with substantial scholarly training in the New Testament who for personal or ideological reasons do not take part in the society's activities.

And even the number *two hundred* is somewhat misleading, since it includes all those who were part of the Seminar's proceedings in any fashion- by receiving its mailings, for example, or reading its reports. A truer estimate of the number of participants who met regularly, wrote papers, and voted on decisions, is closer to forty. The Seminar's climatic publication *The Five Gospels* lists seventy-four "fellows" of the seminar. The number alone suggests that any claim to represent "scholarship" or the academy is ludicrous.[11]

QUESTIONS FOR REVIEW REFLECTION, AND DISCUSSION

1. What is a "straw man"?

2. What is the straw man used by liberal Christianity concerning the interpretation of the Bible?

3. Is choosing between a literal interpretation of the Bible and a historical critical interpretation of the Bible necessary and/or helpful? Why or why not?

4. What is Sallie McFague's understanding of the theology for our day? What might be some of the consequences of her conclusions?

---

11. Johnson, *Real Jesus*, 2–3.

5. What is the basic conclusion of the Jesus Seminar and the quest for Jesus movement concerning the canonical Gospels?
6. What is Werner H. Kebler's conclusion towards the disciples as found in his book *Mark's Story of Jesus*?

Women's Rights and the Bible

*A Samaritan woman came to draw water, and
Jesus said to her, "Give me a drink."*

JOHN 4:7

IN HIS BOOK *What Paul Really Said About Women: An Apostle's Liberating Views on Equality, in Marriage, Leadership, and Love*, John Temple Bristow gives a classic straw man argument. Bristow begins his book with the statement, "Throughout most of church history, the apostle Paul has held the reputation of being what one might call the Great Christian Male Chauvinist toward women".[1]

The statement written by Dr. Bristow, a pastor serving in the Disciples of Christ Church, a liberal voice in the Christian choir, effectively defines the parameters of the book and his argument as it is presented. However, it creates a very narrow, culturally bound picture of women's rights. Further, it creates an in-group with those who agree with his statement or *want* to agree with his statement and then an out-group with those who are then given the label "male chauvinist."

Dr. Bristow seems unwilling or unable to acknowledge that his own understanding of equality toward women is based on equality as understood in the United States in current times. It assumes that access equals equality. Access and equality are very important principles when considering who is eligible to vote or

1. Bristow, *What Paul Really Said*, 1.

who is eligible for a job promotion. However, as we will see, it is a much smaller vision of equality than that found in the gospel of Jesus Christ.

Equality as understood in the gospel of Jesus Christ is universal (meaning meant for all) since it is based on two biblical principles. First, God is the Creator of us all and, as a result, each person has value and dignity that is not given by human authority, but rather is a truth given directly from God. (John 1:9 states, "The true light, that enlightens everyone, was coming into the world.") Second, all persons fail and sin and are in need of God's abounding free, responsible grace.

The apostle Paul writes in the book of Rom 1:16–18, "For I am not ashamed of the gospel; it is the power of God for salvation to everyone who has faith, to the Jews first and also to the Greek. For in it the righteousness of God is revealed through faith for faith; as it is written, 'The one who is righteous will live by faith.'"

In this light, we are able to understand that there is a vast breadth within the body of Christ and its understanding of women's rights. At the same time, we are able to uplift the good news that Jesus fundamentally changed and changes the rights of women!

There are basically three views of women found in the Bible and Jesus's interactions with women. At the same time is the fact that Jesus interacted with women all the time. In Jesus's day, to treat a woman as an equal would have been absurd! (And, in truth, in many un-Christianized places within the world this basic premise remains the norm.)

All a person needs to do is pick up a daily paper to find out that there are still areas in the world where girls are not allowed to go to school and learn to read and write. In his book *The New Faces of Christianity: Believing in the Bible in the Global South*, Philip Jenkins gives the following illustration for how the Bible is fundamentally "changing the status of women in places where women are thought of as 'property' or 'inferior' to men."

Jenkins writes,

Do You Still Believe in Miracles?

At one of Zimbabwe's night vigils, a woman preacher drew extraordinary lessons from an unpromising text, the story of Jesus ordering his disciples to untie a donkey for entry into Jerusalem. She applied the passage directly to the experience of African women: "I have seen that we are the donkey spoken of by the Lord . . . Some are even sold. To be married to a man-to be sold! But with the coming of Jesus we are free . . . We were made righteous by Jesus, mothers." Another woman agreed: "I have heard another woman give an example of a donkey that was set free. In coming here to Maronda Mashanu I also have been set free. Thank you, people of God!" This story illustrates themes that we find across much of the global South, namely that women find in the churches the power to speak and often to lead, and that Christianity is transforming women's role and aspirations.[2]

Within the Christian community, equality between men and women is a given, and how that is then lived out within the Christian life can be different. One biblical viewpoint (like within Bristow's thinking), equal access to the various roles in society is understood as an important component in equality. Christians working from this perspective might advocate for women to take an active role in politics and whatever career pursuit they desire, including the ordination of women as clergy and bishops.

The Most Rev. Dr. Katharine Jefferts Schori of the Episcopalian Church in the United States, is a good example of persons holding this viewpoint. These Christians draw heavily on passages like the Samaritan woman found in the fourth chapter of the Gospel of John. If discipleship is understood as leading others to Jesus so that others can also know and understand the truth in Jesus, then the Samaritan woman would be a disciple. John 4:39–42 reads,

> Many Samaritans from the city believed in him because of the woman's testimony, "He told me everything I had done." So when the Samaritans came to him, they asked him to stay with them; and he stayed there two days. And

---

2. Jenkins, *New Faces of Christianity*, 158.

many more believed because of his word. They said to the woman, "It is no longer because of what you have said that we believe, for we have heard for ourselves, and we know that this is truly the Savior of the world."

A second passage is the story of Mary and Martha (Luke 10:38–42) where Mary sat at the feet of Jesus and listened to his teachings. To sit at a teacher's feet would be the position of a learner or even disciple. Therefore, some conclude that Jesus is welcoming Mary as a disciple since he allows her to take the place of a disciple learning at his feet.

For some within the Christian community, equality between men and women is a given and scripture gives us roles that men and women are to pursue. These roles, within the biblical viewpoint, can be understood differently. These biblical premises are built upon the dignity of all people and the thought that scripture gives us the best understanding for how these relationships, including the relationship between husband and wives, are to work. This view recognizes there will naturally be a wide diversity of faithful Christian expression as these relationships built upon common dignity and human value are lived out.

Joyce Meyer is a wonderful example of a woman living life to the fullest within this voice of the Christian family. She is a wonderful teacher, preacher, and speaker, who consistently uplifts the word of God as a gift to God's people. She travels the world and is a blessing to countless women (and men) as she builds up the family of God.

For some within the Christian community, equality between men and women is a given. Each individual is seen as a gift from God. Each is invited to commune with God as they are drawn toward God. Each is encouraged to pursue intellectual challenges—to write, to dream, to pray, to take care of another—while at the same time, access to certain positions are limited. Priests and nuns in the Roman Catholic Church are an example of this. Jesus called twelve men to be his apostles (Matt 10:1–4, Mark 3:12–19, Luke 6:12–16) and at the same time Jesus talked to women all the time. Because of this, it is believed equality is maintained by men and women fulfilling various roles that then uplift and build up the family of God.

Mary the mother of Jesus, seen as *first disciple* in the Gospel of John 2:1–11, gives an example of one who believes. She is the mother of Jesus, therefore, motherhood is understood as a precious gift from God. The mother is one who nurtures, models compassion, and treasures in their hearts gifts from God and from their children (Luke 2:19). Women in the mystical tradition of the church have made a long and meaningful contribution to the life of the Christian community throughout the ages. The book *Christian Mystics: Their Lives and Legacies throughout the Ages* is a wonderful introduction.

A broad view of the Christian family reveals that even though there is agreement that Jesus fundamentally changed attitudes toward women for all time and that Christians are in basic agreement concerning the equality of men and women in the eyes of God, there is still much for the Christian to talk about and debate. The debate is about the Bible, the teachings of Jesus, the traditions of the church, and the amazing witness and contributions of believers throughout the ages understood as authoritative.

This gives us a much broader and deeper vision than that given by Dr. Bristow, a vision that embraces the vast differences in Christian expression. As I will discuss later in this book, this broader, deeper, authoritative vision is not always maintained in some of the issues discussed extensively within liberal Christian churches.

Finally, it does not appear that there is a voice within the Christian family toward women that guarantees or detracts Christian women from positions of leadership. For every Hillary Clinton or Janet Reno there is a Condoleezza Rice or Sarah Palin. Each of these Christian women have made contributions for the greater good and achieved very high leadership positions. Each woman makes their spiritual home in a different voice within the Christian choir. Yet, the *inherent* God-given value and dignity of each one is known, in truth, as a given.

QUESTIONS FOR REVIEW REFLECTION, AND DISCUSSION

1. What is the understanding of equality espoused by Dr. Bristow and much of today's liberal Christian church? How is this different from equality as understood in the gospels of Jesus Christ?
2. What can be the result of "access equals equality"?
3. How does Jesus fundamentally change the rights of women for all time?
4. What is your understanding of women's rights and the Bible? How do you try to live this out?

Inclusiveness and Universality

I am the true vine, and my father is the vinegrower. He removes every branch in me that bears no fruit. Every branch that bears fruit he prunes to make it bear more fruit.

JOHN 15:1

IN LIBERAL CHRISTIANITY, THE concept of *inclusiveness* has replaced the concept of *universality*. Inclusiveness is usually defined as attempting to reach out to the outcast or those seen as out of the mainstream. In this way, the motives might be virtuous, however, the scope of the mission field and how to best minister to those in the mission field changes.

First of all, by definition, the concept of inclusion means that others are now excluded. Those groups deemed as included and those deemed as excluded can change. However, in reality, the inclusion/exclusion parameters *need* each other to remain viable. Further, to include another means that the in group must create how they will now include those they had previously excluded. A perfect example of this scenario playing itself out in the liberal church is the debate that occurs around the ordination of women. As I have already discussed in the previous chapter, this is a biblical debate and there are a variety of faithful and valid Christian expressions.

The biblical concept of inclusion is based on universality. In this regard, all persons (emphasis on "all") are included in the same way. There is no exclusion because all are fundamentally created by God and in need of God's grace. Therefore universality is not a concept that is man-made but rather from a biblical perspective is a gift from God!

With this as a backdrop, I decided to explore membership trends among twelve denominations in the United States. John 15:1 uplifts Jesus as the vine, therefore it is reasonable to conclude that God will bless faithfulness; that in situations where Christian communities seek to remain attached to the vine through word, tradition, witness, study, reason, and prayer, then God will continue to prune that community so that it can continue to produce fruit and in practical terms grow in membership. Further, it follows that if a Christian community chooses to detach itself from the living vine of Christ, then that community will slowly wither and, again in practical terms, lose members.

Time and time again, Christian history has demonstrated the power of revival and reformation, when communities of faith that have drifted away or chosen to detach themselves from Christ are revitalized and even refused to the vine of Christ by God's mercy and faithfulness, thus demonstrating new abundance and life and membership growth. It is my prayer that this will happen in my own United Methodist Church family.

Since I am taking the premise that God is active and alive in the life of Christian communities, then it follows that a survey of membership trends can decipher God's activity and presence among us. Finally, since God is faithful, a loss of membership within a denomination *does not* mean that those within are unloved by God or are somehow less Christian. No, what it means is that God will continue to meet faithfulness with faithfulness and bless the lives of individuals; however, as a corporate Christian family, God will allow withering and death when it has chosen to somehow remove itself from the universal, free, responsible grace that is the cross of Christ.

To do this, I chose twelve denominations. Initially, I wanted to explore the effect of women's ordination so there are nine denominations that ordain women and three that do not. Second, the trends are dramatic. This then requires further investigation.

Do You Still Believe in Miracles?

The denominations selected for the survey are the African Methodist Episcopal Zion Church, American Baptist Church USA, Assemblies of God, Christian Church (Disciples of Christ), Church of the Nazarene, Episcopal Church in the United States, Presbyterian Church in America, Presbyterian Church USA, Roman Catholic Church, Southern Baptist Convention, United Church of Christ, and the United Methodist Church.

Admittedly, personal curiosity as a pastor in the evangelical Wesleyan tradition is the reason I chose three Wesleyan-rooted denominations; the African Methodist Episcopal Zion Church, Church of the Nazarene, and the United Methodist Church. Also, I chose to examine both the Presbyterian Church in America and the Presbyterian Church USA because this denomination split in 1973 was largely based on the ordination of women.[1]

	1995[2]	Most Current[3]
African Methodist Episcopal Zion Church	1,200,000	1,430,795 (2002)
American Baptist Church USA	1,537,400	1,400,000 (2004)
Assemblies of God	2,257,846	2,687,266 (2002)
Christian Church (Disciples of Christ)	1,022,926	786,334 (2002)
Church of the Nazarene	591,134	639,330 (2002)
Episcopalian Church in the United States	2,471,880	2,320,221 (2002)
Presbyterian Church in America	197,591	310,750 (2002)
Presbyterian Church USA	3,700,000	2,525,330 (2000)
Roman Catholic Church	59,221,000	67,515,016 (2007)
Southern Baptist Convention	15,365,486	16,247,736 (2002)
United Church of Christ	1,555,382	1.330.985 (2002)
United Methodist Church	8,650,388	8,251,042 (2002)

1. Mead, *Handbook* 12th ed., 140–41.
2. Mead, *Handbook* 10th ed.
3. Mead, *Handbook* 12th ed.

The first thing one notices within this survey is that there are many denominations in the United States that are growing in members. God is active and the body of Christ continues to know situations of thriving and vitality. Also, it is clear that there are communities in the Christian family that are declining in membership and showing signs of withering and lack of vitality.

The African Methodist Episcopal Zion Church, Assemblies of God, Church of the Nazarene, Presbyterian Church in America, Roman Catholic Church and Southern Baptist Convention are growing. The American Baptist Church USA, Christian Church (Disciples of Christ), Episcopalian Church in the United States, Presbyterian Church USA, United Church of Christ and the United Methodist Church are all declining in membership.

If we take the idea of women ordained as pastors to be a "liberal" position within the church family we can deduce that most Christians currently choose to worship in a church denomination where women are not ordained. At the same time, it is apparent that women's ordination is not a clear indicator of church membership growth.

This would be consistent with the idea that it is a biblical debate. Therefore, it is a form of Christian expression that continues to remain linked to the vine of Christ and is blessed with growth and vitality.

The African Methodist Episcopal Zion Church (AME Zion Church), American Baptist Church USA, Assemblies of God, Christian Church (Disciples of Christ), Church of the Nazarene, Episcopalian Church in the United States, Presbyterian Church USA, the United Church of Christ, and the United Methodist Church all ordain women. The African Methodist Episcopal Zion Church, Assemblies of God and Church of the Nazarene are all demonstrating membership growth. However, the rest are experiencing membership decline.

Therefore, the question becomes, "Is there a common theological path that these six denominations have taken?" Is there a fork in thinking that has led away from the vine of Christ? Is there a common decision made where the choice has been to detach itself from tradition, word, and witness of the Body of Christ throughout the ages. The answer is, "Yes!"

Now it is to this fork in the road that we turn to next . . .

QUESTIONS FOR REVIEW REFLECTION, AND DISCUSSION

1. How has liberal Christianity replaced universality with inclusiveness and what are some of the natural consequences?

2. Does a loss in church membership at a denominational level mean that those within that denomination are unloved by God or are somehow less Christian?

3. What are some of your experiences with inclusiveness? Have you experienced these situations in positive or negative ways? Explain.

4. Did all denominations surveyed that ordain women lose membership? What would this suggest?

Abortion and Truth

For it was you who formed my inward parts; you knit me together in my mother's womb. I praise you, for I am fearfully and wonderfully made. Wonderful are your works that I know very well.

Psalm 139:13–14

My first experience of a Christian attempt to justify abortion occurred in seminary. Once again, it was the class on Christology, the class where we were not taught about the Trinity because the professor found it to be unconvincing.

In the class we had to read four books and write a paper discussing each book. The books were *Models of God: Theology for an Ecological, Nuclear Age* written by Sallie McFague, *The Color of God: The Concept of God in Afro-American Thought* written by Major J. Jones, *The God of Life* written by Gustavo Gutierrez, and *Omnipotence and Other Theological Mistakes* written by Charles Hartshorne.

At first, I thought we were being exposed to a wide range of Christian concepts to broaden our understanding as we prepared to be pastors. I also thought that those examples of stepping outside of the biblical witness were done so we would know how to talk to a person in our ministry that might be living this way. Soon however, it was apparent that the professor agreed with McFague and Hartshorne.

Do You Still Believe in Miracles?

To my amazement and dismay, I must admit that this type of thinking is all over the place in my United Methodist denomination. It is apparent both at the top end of the hierarchy and at the lay level, though at the lay level the individual rarely realizes that their perspective no longer uses the Bible, church tradition and Christian witness throughout the ages to be authoritative. Instead, they begin with a personal feeling or thought and then fill in the "theological" or "philosophical" reasoning later.

This type of rationalization, particularly with subjects such as abortion, happens all the time. It is one of the most emotional issues of our day. But when you boil it down, abortion is either a great step forward for human civilization or it is a terrible crime against humanity.

Like most people today, I was not attuned to the abortion debate when the Roe v. Wade verdict occurred. In 1973, I was eight years old, so I am unable to understand the emotion of "back alley" abortions. I do, however, know very well the great impact of legalized abortion.

The theological and philosophical foundations of abortion stand *outside* the Christian church tradition and biblical witness. This is not said in an attempt to be mean or try to belittle a person with this foundation. It is simply an attempt to state truth. This is a truth stated very clearly by both McFague and Hartshorne. These Christian thinkers have chosen to think outside of the box. It is said very clearly within their writings and it is a decision of which they seem to be very proud.

As stated in the chapter "The Quest for Christ and the Reality of Jesus," McFague writes that "theology must be self-consciously constructive, willing to think differently than in the past."[1] Later she wrote,

> Theology in our day needs to be self-consciously constructive in order to free itself from traditional notions of divine sovereignty sufficiently to be able to experiment with other and more appropriate metaphors and models that may help us cope with the "question now before the

---

1. McFague, *Models of God*, 21.

human species . . . whether life or death will prevail on earth."[2]

In his book *Omnipotence and Other Theological Mistakes*, Hartshorne (a process theologian) begins,

> In this section I introduce, with a minimum of criticism or argument, six ideas about God which have been held by a great number of learned and brilliant philosophers and theologians through many centuries and in many religious traditions, but which I and many others, including some distinguished modern theologians and philosophers have found quite unacceptable. In other words, what we attack is an old tradition, but we *attack* it standing within somewhat a newer tradition.
>
> In this newer tradition there is a partial appeal (with reservations) to still a third tradition which is old indeed, expressed in various writings, including the Old and New Testaments of the Bible. For it is our contention that the "theological mistakes" in question give the word *God* a meaning which is not true to its import in sacred writings or in concrete religious piety. This result came about partly because theologians in medieval Europe and the Near East were somewhat learned in Greek philosophy and largely ignorant of any other philosophy. This happens in both Christianity and Islam, to a somewhat lesser extent Judaism. In all three religions there was a development of mysticism, which was different still and in some ways partially corrective of the all-too Greek form taken by official theologies.[3]

Hartshorne then identifies the six theological mistakes. First mistake: God is absolutely perfect and therefore unchangeable. Second mistake: omnipotence. Third mistake: omniscience. Fourth mistake: God's unsympathetic goodness. Fifth mistake:

---

2. McFague, *Models of God*, 21.
3. Hartshorne, *Omnipotence*, 1.

immorality as a career after death. Sixth mistake: revelation as infallible.[4]

It is easy to see that God as understood throughout Christian tradition and in the biblical account is no longer recognizable. Free, universal, responsible grace given through the cross and resurrection is gone! Abortion demonstrating a universal understanding of life as a gift is no longer a given.

When discussing abortion, something Hartshorne does at length, he writes,

> The aliveness and humanity of a fetus, meaning its origin in, and (given sufficient help) likely development into human adulthood is admitted by all parties. The question, however, concerns, not the value of the origin, or the possible eventual stage of development, of the fetus, but the value of the actual stage. Not everything that can be is, and the "equal value of the actual and the possible" is not an axiom that anybody lives by or could live by. Many things in an early stage of development would have an importance in later stage which they lack in their earliest stages. In nearly every society until recent centuries, it was taken for granted that killing of human adults is vastly more serious matter than even infanticide (if the latter be done by the parent or parents). This is enough to show the idea of a fetus as a person in the full sense is not so plainly true that it can be used as a noncontroversial premise for political or moral conclusions.[5]

In his book *The Gospel of Life*, written by Pope John Paul II, the Christian tradition of the church (something Hartshorne has self-consciously chosen to depart) is stated. Pope John Paul II writes,

> *Christian Tradition* as the *Declaration* issued by the Congregation for the Doctrine of the Faith points out so well-is clear and unanimous, from the beginning up to our own day, in describing abortion as a particularly grave moral disorder. From its first contacts with the

---

4. Hartshorne, *Omnipotence*, 2–6.
5. Hartshorne, *Omnipotence*, 101.

Greco-Roman world, where abortion and infanticide were widely practiced, the first Christian community, by its teaching and practice, radically opposed the customs rampant in the society, as is shown in the *Didache* mentioned earlier.

Among the Greek ecclesiastical writers, Athenagoras records that Christians consider as murderesses women who have recourse to abortifacient medicines, because children, even if they are still in their mother's womb, "are already under the protection of Divine Providence." Among the Latin authors, Tertullian affirms: "It is anticipated murder to prevent someone from being born; it makes little difference whether or kills a soul already born or puts it to death at birth. He who will one day be a man is a man already."

Throughout Christianity's two thousand year history, this same doctrine has been constantly taught by the Fathers of the Church and by her Pastors and Doctors even scientific and philosophical discussions about the precise moment of the infusion of the spiritual soul have never given rise to any hesitation about the moral condemnation of abortion.[6]

When life begins within Hartshorne's framework is very difficult to pinpoint, though fluent speech and reasoning is mentioned many times. Hartshorne writes, "We should all be 'for life,' especially for the lives of those who are quite certainly persons."[7] I for one want no part in trying to distinguish "quite certainly persons" from "not quite" persons.

By contrast Pope John Paul II clearly states,

> Life is indelibly marked by a *truth of its own*. By accepting God's gift, man is obliged to *maintain life in this truth* which is essential to it. To detach oneself from this truth is to condemn oneself to meaningless and unhappiness, and possibly to become a threat to the existence of others, since the barriers guaranteeing respect for life and

---

6. John Paul II, *Gospel of Life*, 109–10.
7. Hartshorne, *Omnipotence*, 102.

the defense of life, in every circumstance, have been broken down.[8]

Following the premise articulated in the previous chapter, that God will bless and grow Christian communities that are attached to the living vine of Christ and that God will allow Christian communities to wither and even die when the community has chosen to detach itself from the Bible, Christian tradition, and Christian witness, I decided to take the same twelve denominations and analyze another fork in the road of thought and Christian practice.

Currently, there are six denominations that are listed as members of the Religious Coalition of Reproductive Choice. The organization's stated position states,

> Diverse religious denominations and traditions compassionately affirm a woman's moral right to make reproductive decisions according to her conscience and religious principles. Major faith organizations representing millions of Americans have long supported a woman's right to choose. In keeping with our nation's constitutional guarantee of religion, they oppose civil laws that would impose specific religious views about abortion on all Americans.[9]

The Religious Coalition for Productive Choice has defended the procedure called "partial birth abortion" and opposed attempts to litigate parental notification. The six denominations (the only six denominations) listed as members of the religious Coalition for Reproductive Choice are American Baptist USA, Christian Church (Disciples of Christ), Episcopal Church, Presbyterian Church USA, United Church of Christ and the United Methodist Church. When analyzing membership trends, I chose to begin in the early 1970s since abortion became legal in the United States in 1973. Below is a record of my findings.

---

8. John Paul II, *Gospel of Life*, 84.

9. www.rcrc.org. Author's Note: Some of the research for this book was conducted in 2008; as a result, many of the specific URLs for the information reported are unavailable at the time of publication.

ABORTION AND TRUTH

	1975[10]	Most Current
American Baptist Church USA	1,562,740	1,400,000[11] (2004)
Christian Church (Disciples of Christ)	1,356,914	786,334[12] (2002)
Episcopal Church	3,062,734	2,320,221[13] (2002)
Presbyterian Church USA	2,908,958	2,525,330[14] (2000)
United Church of Christ	1,859,016	1,330,985[15] (2002)
United Methodist Church	10,334,521	8,251,042[16] (2002)

This survey of membership shows a significant decline in membership in every denomination that is a member of the Religious Coalition for Reproductive Choice. By their association with the coalition, these denominations indicate a support of abortion rights. In the early 1970s, the total membership among these six denominations was 21,084,883. The total membership among these six denominations in the most current column is 16,611,912. This is a combined loss in membership of nearly five million members or around 21 percent reduction in membership. These figures are even more staggering when you consider the overall growth in population within the United States. The 1970 population in the United States was 203,302,031 and in 2008 it is estimated to be 303,824,640 persons.[17]

Using the same line of thinking, let us look at the other six denominations examined earlier. The membership trends from the

10. Mead, *Handbook* 6th ed.
11. Grossman, "Some Protestant Churches."
12. Mead, *Handbook* 12th ed.
13. Mead, *Handbook* 12th ed.
14. http://eee.accsd.org/Presbyterian.html.
15. Mead, *Handbook* 12th ed.
16. Mead, *Handbook* 12th ed.
17. "25-Year Table."

1970s to today for the African Methodist Episcopal Zion Church, Assemblies of God, Church of the Nazarene, Presbyterian Church in America, Roman Catholic Church, and Southern Baptist Convention follow.

	1975[18]	Most Current
African Methodist Episcopal Zion Church (AME Zion Church)	1,342,427	1,430,795[19] (2002)
Assemblies of God	1,099,606	2,687,266[20] (2002)
Church of the Nazarene	404,732	639,330[21] (2002)
Presbyterian Church in America	organized in 1973	310,750[22] (2002)
Roman Catholic Church	48,390,990	67,515,016[23] (2007)
Southern Baptist Convention	12,067,284	16,247,736[24] (2002)

The first thing one may notice is that each of these denominations has known membership growth since the early 1970s. In fact, membership growth is dramatic. Over twenty five million, five hundred members! That bears repeating! Over 25,500,000 members. Clearly, God is active and blessing these denominations. The total membership within these denominations in the early 1970s was 63,305,039, and the figure in the most current survey is 88,830,893 members. This is a gain of a little over 28 percent membership!

To put it simply, the religious Coalition for Reproductive Choice is strongly overstating their position when they state that

---

18. Mead, *Handbook* 6th ed.
19. Mead, *Handbook* 12th ed.
20. Mead, *Handbook* 12th ed.
21. Mead, *Handbook* 12th ed.
22. Mead, *Handbook* 12th ed.
23. Bunson, *Our Sunday Visitor's Almanac.*
24. Mead, *Handbook* 12th ed.

they represent "diverse religious denominations and traditions."[25] In reality, this group represents a very small number of Christian denominations in this country and a very small membership. Currently, there are over 250 denominations in the United States representing well over two hundred million persons.[26]

It seems that this overstating of one's own position (as observed earlier when discussing the Jesus Seminar) has become something of a trend.

Membership trends will be revisited in part two of this book, in the chapter "Grace and Truth," which will explore membership at or around 2025.

---

25. www.rcrc.org.
26. Mead, *Handbook* 12th ed.

Popularity, Comfort, and Blindness

He has told you, O mortal what is good; and what does the Lord require of you but to do justice, and to love kindness, and to walk humbly with your God.

Micah 6:8

Everyone likes to be liked. To be told they are valued and important. Everyone wants to have a place, a circle of friends or family where they feel popular.

In American culture, being popular is held in very high regard. For a number of years, *American Idol* has been the number one show on TV, as millions vote for the singer they like the best.

There is nothing innately wrong with the desire of popularity; however, if made an end in itself, it can have a difficult, if not disastrous effect. We vote for our elected officials (a form of popularity contest), and unstated in the arrangement is the basic idea that what a candidate says and what they do will be the same. In other words, saying something to be popular and then doing something very different is usually understood as a negative thing.

Often, the desire to be popular can be a difficult challenge for a church pastor and even the church in its institutional forms. The basic idea expressed by many is something like this: "Don't talk about things that make people uncomfortable. If you do, it might hurt church attendance (and ultimately church offerings)."

POPULARITY, COMFORT, AND BLINDNESS

We live in a society that likes to be comfortable. Who doesn't like to be comfortable? We like to have popcorn ready in two or three minutes, movies that stream into our homes on demand, and cell phones that give us access to the internet whenever and wherever we are. Being popular and having a desire to remain comfortable are often wedded together. However, this is not the role of the Christian church. Rather, there are times when the church and the church faithful who seek to live out their faith in their daily lives must shed light on things that make us uncomfortable or upset.

Shedding light on individual and/or societal blindness is not popular or a comfortable thing to do. Yet there are times it is the responsibility and role of the church and the call of Christian individuals to shed difficult light that is unpopular and rattle us from the comforts of popularity to then claim true hope, joy and peace that is known in Christ.

For nearly two years now I have worked as a hospital chaplain at a trauma 1 inner-city hospital. This means that the most severe trauma patients are funneled to this hospital. Car wrecks, gun shot wounds, stabbings, assaults, accidents (you name it) are seen on a daily basis. It is a very challenging position and a ministry that has brought me to tears and the solace of private prayer many times. One of the main roles of a chaplain in this type of setting is to meet parents, friends, and family who have rushed to the hospital after hearing that their loved one has been brought there. Another role is to be with families and friends at the death of a loved one or to be there within five minutes of a person dying.

In these moments, the chaplain is called to simply stand as a caring presence; to stand and be with persons in the midst of the truth of human fear, anguish, and grief. There is truth in human fear, anguish, and grief; even Jesus wept (John 11:35).

Oftentimes when I am in these situations, persons of faith ask me to pray and in these sacred moments, I seek to remind all gathered of the need to stand in truth. For the Christian, this means God is God. That human grief and anguish is real. And during times when we are disoriented, it is important to stand in truth; the truth that this person is loved, the truth of the pain being experienced, the truth of the comfort known in God that is experienced by countless persons, the truth of family and friends.

As a chaplain, I have been called to be with parents, friends, and families in the midst of tragedies and societal ills that can be a real party downer. Who wants to hear about heroin addiction, domestic abuse, and inner-city gun violence? These topics make us uncomfortable. Yet, there are times when we *must* talk about these concerns because only by bringing these topics into the open can truth be heard and change occur.

Three times I have been with family and friends who stood next to the bed of a young adult who has accidentally overdosed on heroin. These were not young adults who wanted to die. Yet heroin is unpredictable and can have evil consequences. In these situations, there has been an extra layer of grief experienced by all. How could this happen? How did they get the drugs? Who gave them the drugs? Why did this happen? They were looking forward to that new job. They weren't depressed. They were trying to get into rehab. Why didn't they think? Why did this happen?

I have met with persons who have been victimized by domestic abuse. Often comments like "It's never been this bad" or "He's only like this when he's been drinking" or "He's been depressed since he lost his job" are heard. These are all foundations for potential change if they are statements of truth and if change is something that is truly desired. Without these statements, without light that is shed on the truth of the situation, the violence is going to continue. Shedding light and truth is a necessary step that can lead to healing and transformation.

Inner-city violence and violence among men (ages 17–30) make me uncomfortable. Yet, the number of times I have been in the trauma bay when a young man has been shot is staggering. On one weekend, I was with the family of a seventeen-year-old man on a Saturday and an eighteen-year-old man on a Sunday. Tremendous grief and anger was experienced by family and friends. Both situations were random, where the victim was not sought out but rather was simply in the wrong place at the wrong time, a victim of random violence. The frustration, anger, and helplessness of the parents of these young men have deeply touched my heart, have led me to solace in private prayer and indirectly inspired this chapter focused on popularity, comfort and blindness.

There are times when Christian individuals, pastors, and institutions must risk challenging the comfort level of our society, of being unpopular. As Christians, we know the truth of living hope (I Pet 1:3) and believe in individual and societal transformation through Christ. Christian hope is rooted in the power of light and the One who is the living hope, Jesus the Son of God.

Christian history is sprinkled with those who were unpopular, and shook the foundations of comfort by simply shedding light and truth upon societal blindness. This light and truth upon societal blindness resulted in transformation and change that previously had been unimaginable. William Wilberforce was such a Christian man, who lived from 1759 to 1833 in England. He was a politician and a member of parliament who worked to abolish slavery in England and throughout the British Empire. This was a very unpopular position to espouse at that time, and yet Wilberforce saw it as a societal ill that had a negative effect on all in his society. In his book *Real Christianity*, Wilberforce wrote,

> We often choose reputation over obedience. When earthly reward is the highest value to us and worldly shame is viewed as the greatest off all possible evils, we are prone to change the course of our obligations to God and seek a way to do them that avoids the natural consequences of taking a stand against the cultural norm.[1]

Nelson Mandela was a Christian man deeply rooted in Wesleyan thought. As a boy, he attended a Wesleyan missionary school and later the Wesleyan college of Fort Beaufort. Mandela saw that the sin of apartheid affected all. He worked to end apartheid and even spent twenty-seven years of his life in a South African jail, Yet today, South Africa lives in the truth of what was unimaginable and is free from apartheid.

---

1. Wilberforce, *Real Christianity*, 88.

Do You **Still** Believe in Miracles?

Mother Teresa was a Christian woman who sought to minister and demonstrate the love of God among the poor, helpless, and dying. She took an unpopular position of shedding light upon the condition of the Dalit people of India, also known as the "untouchables." Shedding light upon their poverty and chronic oppression was difficult to see and shook people out of their comfort zone. However, her work and witness and the movement the Missionaries of Charity, which she helped start, has given voice and hope to the poor, not only in India but throughout the world.

Oscar Romero was a Christian man who spoke for the poor and oppressed indigenous people of El Salvador. This was an unpopular position and unsettled the ruling elite from their comfort zone. At times, living and even governing in a certain way because it has always been done that way does not mean it is a just way or that it cannot know transformation, healing, and new life. Even in death Archbishop Oscar Romero, known as "the bishop of the poor," continues to leave a legacy of hope and the possibility of change to countless persons.

As a local pastor, it would have been so much easier to not talk about abortion. In my United Methodist denomination, our official position is to respect a woman's right to choose and also uplift the sanctity of life. This is a very difficult balance and sometimes can feel like it is trying to have it all and actually being left with very little. The position attempts to uplift that there are a variety of perspectives within the denomination and hold these in creative tension. However, many times this means do not rock the boat, so do not talk about it. Yet there are many times we must talk about those things that make us uncomfortable and shed light on things that make us sick to our stomachs. For in addressing the truth of our day, we open ourselves up to change, healing, and transformation.

Many years ago, William Wilberforce wrote these words, which speak truth and challenge us today. Wilberforce wrote,

> What is good is only a matter of opinion in a secular society, Using society's own standards of goodness, careful observation of the bigger picture may reveal that a

particular good has been outweighed by general evil. When a society defines its own morality and then applies it to itself, that society can justify its own serious breaches of character. It is able to lower that standard to the detriment of all.[2]

QUESTIONS FOR REVIEW REFLECTION, AND DISCUSSION

1. In your own words, why is shedding light on individual and/or societal blindness a necessary role of the Christian church? Give examples either from the book or your own experience.

2. William Wilberforce wrote, "What is good is only a matter of opinion in a secular society. Using society's standards of goodness, careful observation of the bigger picture may reveal that a particular good has been outweighed by a general evil. When a society defines its own morality and then applies it to itself, that society can justify its own serious breaches of character. It is able to lower to the detriment of all." Do Wilberforce's words still apply to today's realities? Why or why not?

---

2. Wilberforce, *Real Christianity*, 99.

Do No Harm

*Come all who are weary and heavy
laden and I will give you rest.*

MATTHEW 11:28

DO NO HARM!

It seems that at every ministerial gathering I have attended over the past few years I have heard this phrase, "Do No Harm." At first glance, this statement seems straight forward. However, it is with a sense of sadness that I must say that the tone of my own denomination has definitely changed towards those who consider themselves as Bible believing or conservative or orthodox or classical or evangelical or fundamentalist. There seems to be a growing sense of frustration and even *hostility* towards these groups from the more liberal or modern or process oriented or progressive groups within my United Methodist denomination.

My concern is that ideas that I learned in seminary have filtered into the church at all levels. Because of this, there are times that the phrase "Do No Harm" seems like code and is directed towards the Bible believing, conservative or orthodox or classical or evangelical or fundamentalist groups within the church. I realize this might be hard to fathom and I truly believe this was not the case when I started pastoral ministry almost fourteen years ago. However, today the tone is different.

Bishop Robert Schnase of the Missouri Conference of the United Methodist Church expresses this developing tone, which is subtly and not so subtly repeated in countless ways in his book *Five Practices of Fruitful Congregations.* Schnase writes,

> We should never apologize that we pray and work for more people to experience and share our ministry in Christ's name. This desire is unselfish; it is a purpose worth pouring our lives into, and it is the central purpose of the church. To desire more people in our churches does not make us fundamentalist, small-minded, aggressive, strident, or intrusive.[1]

In seminary, I came into contact with the following ideas in a few of the classes I attended. These classes and their instructors would have been very comfortable with the following quote found in Charles Hartshorne's book *Omnipotence and Other Theological Mistakes.*

> Pollsters are telling us that a substantial majority of the citizens of this country believe in God. As a believer, I find this encouraging. In Europe it seems that believers are perhaps a minority. But, alas, I strongly suspect that in Europe literal-minded fundamentalists are a much smaller proportion of believers than in the case here. As a non-literal believer, I find this fact discouraging, almost frightening. Given enough political power to fundamentalists, how closely might we come to a new Inquisition, that great monstrosity which disfigured Traditional Christianity? Religious fanaticism is still with us, and it has an ugly history.
>
> A friend, a theologian, had a phrase that stuck with me, "the acidity of orthodoxy." Orthodoxy can be worse than acid. It can be lethal. I have encountered a "pro-lifer" who gave me little sense of being pro my life or the life of adults generally. Pro-fetus life is a very special enthusiasm for life. I have respect for the fetus as, like all animals, a wondrous creation, and a suitable object

---

1. Schnase, *Five Practices*, 136.

for sympathy. In addition it is capable of eventually, with much help from relatively adults persons, of becoming first an infant (and then a child), beginning to learn from its elders, and finally an adult human person. We are all human *individuals* long before we are *persons* in the value sense of actually thinking and reasoning in the human fashion.[2]

Obviously, this is a straw man argument mixed with fear mongering. Further, it is obvious that intelligent, respectful theological discourse is not sought by the author. Rather, there is the creation of an "us" and "them"; even a "good" and "bad." It is this fork in thought that has been crossed in some situations by persons in the liberal wings of the Christian choir towards those in the more conservative, orthodox, Bible believing, classical, evangelical, fundamentalists wings of the Christian choir. This tragic reality is most evident when discussing abortion and, more specifically, post-abortion syndrome.

I have friends and colleagues—peers who have given tremendous time and energy developing food pantries, supporting Alcoholic Anonymous groups, leading Grief Support groups, Nicotine and Cigarette education, Vacation Bible Schools, etc.—who simply go blank or become very angry when Post Abortion Syndrome is discussed. There are those trying to deny that this is a real condition or belittle the reality of it or get outraged by the mention of it. As a friend, I realize these are early stages of grief. I also observe that colleagues stuck in these early stages of grief can develop depression and many other anti-life affirming outcomes.

These co-workers are good people, many of whom grieved at the result of legalized abortion in the United States. However, they continue to defend women's right to choose out of a misguided loyalty and an inability to see a theological truth that can free them from their own thinking. No one ever thought we would reach over 1,300,000 a year (a little over three thousand daily).[3] These kinds of numbers were inconceivable almost forty years ago. No

---

2. Hartshorne, *Omnipotence*, 116–17.
3. National Right to Life, "Abortion Statistics."

one would have dreamed that experts believe that one of every three girls growing up today will have an abortion by the time they are forty-five.[4]

I know there is a continuing debate concerning post-abortion syndrome. Some report, "The answer is no, 'post-abortion syndrome" doesn't exist."[5] However, even those who do not call it post-abortion syndrome admit that tens of thousands of women experience prolonged negative effects from abortion. This is a figure found in the *New York Times* magazine (hardly a bastion for conservative thought), in an article written by Emily Bazelon titled "Is There a Post-Abortion Syndrome?" Bazelon eventually argues that such a condition does not exist and that "tens of thousands" of women who do experience some type of emotional distress after an abortion are a very small number proportionally to all women who had an abortion.[6] The figure slightly over 50,000 is rather common, while other data suggests more than 500,000[7] and still other data suggests a much, much larger number ranging from seven to twenty million, who are negatively affected by their decision to have an abortion.[8]

My point is not to debate numbers or semantics in diagnosis. Nor am I a politician or a psychiatrist. What I am is a pastor. That means I am called into a healing profession. It is not my choice to minister healing to one person and then deny another that same grace based on their lifestyle choices. I am a pastor. My scope is universal, not inclusive.

While watching the Philadelphia Phillies and the Florida Marlins play in the 2008 World Series, I could not help but think that at the very, very least you could fill the stadium with women suffering from post-abortion syndrome and there would still be women who could not get in. That is a staggering image! As

4. Harris, "Number of Women"; "Get 'in the Know.'"
5. Friedman, "Answer Is No"; "Post-Abortion Syndrome."
6. Bazelon, "Post-Abortion Syndrome."
7. Major, "Pro-Choice Researchers Acknowledge."
8. Major, "Pro-Choice Researchers Acknowledge"; "New Study Links Abortion"; "Abortion Facts, Post-Abortion Syndrome."

pastors, we are called to be in healing ministry with those who are hurting and we are doing a terrible job with these persons.

Those persons who support abortion and those liberal denominations that support the right to choose should be the first ones to make sure that those who suffer from the effects of an abortion are cared for. Further, they should be the first to argue for the education of the young and their families so that young girls and women who choose this path would be taken care of. This would be a rational line of ministry, which is why I see it as stages of grief.

To get angry with a woman who suffers with post-abortion syndrome after an abortion is irrational. To deny the existence of the condition is denial. To pretend that nothing happened and make sure to not tell anyone and everything will be okay is a fantasy.

Regardless of what decision a person makes, that person is left with a difficult reality. Abortion is not an end of a problem but rather one difficult path among many difficult paths. Further, to be told that one must go it alone without the support of loved ones and friends might be considered good advice in days gone by but is hardly helpful thirty-five years into this social experiment.

In my own ministry in the local church I have personally known dozens of persons both women and men who have been a part of an abortion. (I am just one pastor.) If a pastor tells me that they have not met anyone or been in ministry with anyone who has had an abortion, I really must wonder what they are doing! If nearly one third of the population has personal experience with abortion then how could you not meet persons who have been involved with an abortion?[9]

On a few occasions, women and a couple of men have approached me to talk. I think it is because we have anxiety disorders. Many times when you get to talking you find out that there is something familiar in a person that leads you to think that it is okay to share something painful and difficult.

I am diagnosed with post-traumatic stress disorder and believe that ministering with persons with post-abortion syndrome

---

9. Harris, "Number of Women."

is simply part of my ministry.[10] Getting to know many of them and working with them and seeing how they rely on their faith and Jesus to bring something good out of personal pain has been an inspiration.

Post-abortion syndrome is an anxiety disorder that falls under the post-traumatic stress disorder umbrella.[11] The most common ways that a person develops PTSD are war, sexual assault, and child abuse. To deny a person with post-abortion syndrome access to healing *within* the church or to get outraged at these persons or even deny their existence is very similar to other recent tragedies.

It is like denying the existence of PTSD for a soldier returning from war or getting angry at them because they are not tough enough to get over it and get on with their life. It is like blaming a woman that her sexual assault was her fault because she wore her jeans too tight. It is like telling the child that they deserved the abuse they received because it was their fault they spilled the milk.

All of these accusations are lies! A person with PTSD begins a new stage of healing when they are able to identify and name the lie.

To deny a person with post-abortion syndrome the ability to name their condition or limit their access to healing is repeating these kinds of mistakes. We who are in the ministry cannot develop a new form of segregation where we serve only those we agree with or who do not make us uncomfortable.

We who are blessed by God and called to be pastors must be pastors in all situations. We have a universal ministry of healing. Jesus said, "Let all (ALL) who are weak and heavy laden come to me and I will give you rest" (Matt 11:28). Regardless of how we understand abortion, I still believe that there are pastors on all sides of the debate that agree with this.

---

10. Ruiz, *Post Traumatic Stress Disorder.*

11. Edmondson, "From a Doctor's Viewpoint." See also Burke, "Abortion and Post Traumatic."

QUESTIONS FOR REVIEW REFLECTION, AND DISCUSSION

1. What is post-abortion syndrome?

2. Why is there denial and/or anger towards those with post-abortion syndrome by many liberal individuals and liberal Christian denominations?

3. What would be a rational response by those persons who support abortion and those liberal denominations that support a right to choose towards persons who suffer negatively from the effects of an abortion?

4. What are some real life resources that can be given in your area for persons with post-abortion syndrome? Be specific.

New Gnosticism
and the Canonical Bible

So shall my word be that goes forth out of my mouth; it shall not return unto me void, but it shall accomplish that which I please and it shall prosper in the thing where to I sent it.

ISAIAH 55:11

MY FIRST EXPERIENCE WITH modern theology occurred in seminary. The tragic outcome of this theology is ultimately the need for a new canon, a new savior, a new Gnosticism and the entrapment into a new works reality. This is a far different reality than one of life lived within the law of free, universal, responsible grace.

To explain how this occurs I need to explain what modern theology is and for that I turn once again to my seminary experience. Modern theology was a required class at the Methodist Theological School in Ohio when I attended seminary (1993–1996), and it was taught by Professor Jeffrey Hopper. The two required books for the class were written by Professor Hopper.

The purpose is not to belittle or demonize those Christians who have felt a need to pursue similar paths of thinking. Rather, the point is to uplift the work that has been done and the ways that God can work because of us and/or in spite of us. It is also done, in a pastoral way, inviting fellow pilgrims back to the well worn paths of Jesus who is "My Lord and my God!" (John 20:28).

Hopper explains the dimensions and the purpose of modern theology in this way,

> The popular religious practice of telling people what they want to hear is an encouragement to avoid the risk of faith by hiding in false securities, whether the "preacher" realizes this or not. For that reason, such preaching will always be more widely welcomed than serious theological efforts. Seen from the negative side, theology is "iconoclasm" the smashing of idols, where "idol" means anything *other than* God in which we place our basic trust. The smashing of others' idols has some popularity. The smashing of one's own is resisted with every means at one's disposal. This is one of the major reasons why there is so little understanding of modern theology. Most popular religion today is based-albeit superficially- upon pre-modern theologies, and most of it is idolatrous. It is one of the tasks of theology to reveal these facts, so it is hardly surprising that modern theologies are often branded "heretical." More than anything else, such charges are an indication of the great gulf that separates the popular and the pre-modern understandings of the Christian faith from the teachings of the theologians who recognize that citizens of the developed nations today live in terms of a different basic world of experience that that of Christians of the eras in which the various orthodox theologies were formulated- and who seek therefore to reinterpret Christian faith for our understanding.[1]

Later, Hopper writes,

> The acceptance or non-acceptance of historical-critical approaches to the Scriptures is the most obvious point of contrast between modern and pre-modern theologies and would appear to be the most divisive issue within Christianity today.[2]

---

1. Hopper, *Modern Theology I*, 1–2.
2. Hopper, *Modern Theology I*, 3.

Hopper reasserts the purpose of modern theology at the end of his second book, *Understanding Modern Theology II: Reinterpreting Christian Faith for Changing Worlds.*

Hopper writes,

> That there is much idolatrous—rather than faithful—affirmations of such things as eternal life among Christians is no doubt true, and that is why one of the essential tasks of theology is to expose the idolatrous misuse of traditional Christian teaching.
>
> The fact that doctrinal and liturgical formulations are sometimes found to serve idolatry rather than faith does not necessarily mean that they are unsound when proposed. They may well have been very powerful in confronting persons with the affirmation of sovereign graciousness and the challenge to take the risk of faith. Yet, because of the inevitably of anxiety in human existence and of the self-protectiveness of human motivations, it is also inevitable that those formulations will be "domesticated" in the life of the churches. In this case, familiarity may not "breed contempt" but it removes the metaphoric shock and facilitates the sense of that "of course," I know that. The unrecognized motivation to domesticate effective doctrinal and liturgical forms, namely, the anxious self-protective wish to avoid the risk of trusting utterly in grace, is very powerful and very subtle. Religion as a whole is probably the most subtle way of avoiding the risk of faith *precisely because* it is practiced in the supposition that it is an expression of faith. The answer to this inevitable problem is not the abandonment of religion (as many would urge), but the critical struggle against idolatry. The abandonment of all religiousness, which is to say to surrender all human openness (real as well as false) to the grace of God, even if it were possible, would be out another expression of the human pride that leaves us captive to our anxieties and alienations.
>
> The disturbing characteristics of modern theology, though they have come about in response to the cultural revolutions that led to the modern world, are not to be seen only as accommodations to modernity. They are

Do You Still Believe in Miracles?

also, and more importantly *required by the Christian gospel.* Such, at least, is the judgment of modern theologies.[3]

What will become apparent as I continue to explore modern theologies is that there is quite a range of debate within the movement itself. So much of Hopper's stated positions above would be on the conservative end as newly redefined within the framework of modern theologies. At the same time, there is a consensus within the modernist movement for non-miraculous interpretations of the act of God in Jesus. The movement seeks to interpret Christian faith without divine intervention as traditionally understood. One of the things that you find out is that words and phrases within the movement can change in meaning or have multiple meanings since language as described by its followers is dynamic and changing. This is done because it is believed that the modern mind is no longer able to believe and understand miracles in the same ways that have been traditionally known.

All this is uplifting the intent of modern theology. Previously in the chapter "Abortion and Truth," we examined a very similar intent with Hartshorne and process theology.

I hope one realizes that these theologies completely change a traditional or biblical understanding of the incarnation and resurrection of Jesus. These theologies completely change the traditional biblical understanding of Moses and the parting of the Red Sea. They completely change the traditional biblical understanding of the healing accounts found in the current Gospels that are found in your Bible.

This is a very logical outcome and will lead to the issue of authority, the creation of a new Gnosticism, and eventually the loss of a risen Savior and the gift of free grace.

Finally, it is inevitable that with the loss of a risen Savior and the gift of free grace new Gnosticism (said another way, secret knowledge) will lead to a works mentality (as new scriptures need to be created and new saviors formed). It can also lead to a form of groupthink (which is a much, much smaller scope than

---

3. Hopper, *Modern Theology II*, 152.

NEW GNOSTICISM AND THE CANONICAL BIBLE

universality or even inclusiveness) where only those within the group really get it and are thus part of the new enlightened. Hopper explains the use of historical-critical methodology and the development of the twenty-seven books of the New Testament as it now exists. He explains this development in an effort to get behind the canonical biblical witness to the Spirit of the living Christ. Hopper quotes Campenhausen,

> The first known list that agrees completely with the twenty-seven books that came finally to constitute the New Testament canon was in a letter of Athanasius Bishop of Alexandria, in the year 367.
>
> The first generations of Christianity evidently felt no need for a "New Testament." They assumed the authority of Hebrew Scriptures, and they understood themselves to be under the guidance of the risen Lord. They also expected the final judgment to bring this world to an end very soon, so the apostles' memories of the Lord seemed sufficient.
>
> The central factor in all this was Jesus Christ. Therefore, Hebrew Scriptures did not have the same meaning for the Christians as they did for the Jews. Their authority was assumed, but their meaning was in their pointing to Christ, and not as a set of norms for daily living. Thus, "Early Christianity is positively not to be regarded as a 'religion of the book'; it is the religion of the Spirit of the living Christ." (Campenhausen 1968, 62–63).[4]

As Hopper clearly argues, Scripture as we currently have it in our Bibles is not the result of divine inspiration but human creativity and, in some cases, politics. Hopper seems to ignore the idea that just because we might be able to analyze the development of the New Testament canon, it does not mean God was not involved. Rather, for many it is further evidence of God's living presence within the church and the development of the New Testament

---

4. Hopper, *Modern Theology I*, 152–53.

canon. Hopper simply dismissed these ideas as "pre-modern" and with it the traditional witness of the faithful throughout the ages.

Hopper goes on to write,

> The persons who established the limits of the Christian canon lived in times and with assumptions and information very different from our own, and the arguments that influenced them in the determination we inherit are not generally arguments with which we concur.[5]

Later he adds,

> In view of these many discoveries of modern historical research regarding the development of the list of New Testament scriptures, it is hardly surprising that statements such as the following from Schubert Ogden on the New Testament canon are increasingly common among scholars.
>
> It is the product, indeed of the *experientia ecclesiae*, at least in the sense that it emerged only in the course of the church's continuing attempts to control the putative authorities that would control it in relation to the ultimate source of all authority in Christ himself. But, since "popes and councils can err," the canon that thus emerged from the early church's own experience and decisions is and must be open to revision. (Ogden 1976, 249)
>
> Such statements should not be taken to mean authority of the traditional twenty-seven books is being denied or that there is any greater movement under way to remove any of those books from or add to the New Testament.[6]

With Hopper's last comment, he is standing with the conservative aspects of his movement. Let us revisit Hartshorne's book *Omnipotence and other Theological Mistakes*. Hartshorne writes,

> On a less positive note, I believe—with Pierce, Whitehead, D. H. Lawrence (three rather different persons)

---

5. Hopper, *Modern Theology I*, 154.
6. Hopper, *Modern Theology I*, 155.

and my father (different still)—that the book of Revelation is a poor expression of a religion of love, for the very reason these four agreed upon: that is expresses hate, arrogance, resentment, and superstition run riot. It ought, as they held, to have been omitted from the canon. So there we have it—consensus in religion is out of reach. We have to agree to disagree.[7]

A quick trip to your nearest Barnes & Noble will demonstrate a growing array of new scriptures. There is the Gospel of Thomas, the Gospel of Mary Magdalene, the Gospel of Judas, and even the Gospel according to *The Simpsons*, to name a few. These, for some, are understood as equally authoritative to our current Bible and in many cases more authoritative.

It is to the specific struggle of authority within modern theology that I turn to now.

QUESTIONS FOR REVIEW REFLECTION, AND DISCUSSION

1. Where is there consensus within the modernist movement?
2. Why is the natural consequence of a new Gnosticism the development of a new works reality?
3. Why is the natural scope of Gnosticism different than a traditional Christian perspective?
4. Have you come in contact with Gnostic thought? How and what was your experience?

---

7. Hartshorne, *Omnipotence*, 126.

Authority and Freedom

Jesus straightened up and said to her, "Woman, where are they?" Has no one condemned you?" She said, "No one, sir." And Jesus said, "Neither do I condemn you. Go your way, and from now on do not sin again."

JOHN 8:10–11

THE PASSAGE ABOUT THE woman about to be stoned in the gospel of John (John 7:53—8:11) is one of many examples of free, universal, responsible grace in action. Clearly, those who brought this woman caught in adultery believed this woman was beyond the realms of grace. In fact, the passage tells us that "the law of Moses commanded us to stone such women" (John 8:5). However, Jesus, who ushers in a new age of grace and truth (John 1:17b) redefines the limits and nature of the Mosaic Law.

In the age of grace and truth, grace is universal and Jesus tells the crowd, "Let anyone among you who has no sin cast the first stone" (John 8:7). Grace is universal. Further, Jesus confronts the crowd and redefines the nature and scope of grace before he says anything to the woman. For the grace of God is unmerited, it is free. It is a gift from the very essence of God and God's love. For God is Love (1 John 4:8b). Finally, the woman is told, "Neither do I condemn you. Go your own way and from now on sin no more" (John 8:11). With this, Jesus offers the gift of responsible grace and new life.

AUTHORITY AND FREEDOM

Modern theology struggles with the ability to hold onto the paradox of authority and freedom. For this reason, it either embodies relative grace or turns the other direction and becomes a new form of intolerance. The paradox of authority and freedom is the reality that without authority there is chaos and with unrestrained authority there is repression. The apostle Paul understood this very well when he talked about "freedom in Christ" (Gal 5:13–14).

An example of the difficulty with authority is found within Hopper's book, *Understanding Modern Theology II: Reinterpreting Christian Faith for Changing Worlds*. Hopper summarizes the perspective of modern theologians Edward Farley and Peter C. Hodgson, who judge that

> "with the end of mythological thinking about God, the theological foundations of the scripture principle evaporate . . . The house of authority has collapsed, despite the fact that people still try and live in it" (Farley and Hodgson 1985, 76). This judgment, which in varying degrees and expressions is shared by many modern theologians, results from much critical reflection on the historical developments and cultural changes that this work has been describing. It does not, however, indicate agreement with the view that modern theology has no adequate basis for its reinterpretations.
>
> Instead, the collapse of "the house of authority" is not lamented but praised, for it Is the conviction of modern theologians that the kinds of authority claimed by and for the traditional theologies are incompatible with Christian faith (ibid., 61–86). The claims were idolatrous, their effects were oppressive and dehumanizing, their character was contrary to the will manifest in Jesus Christ.[1]

It is important to note debate and disagreement once again *within* modern theology. Similar debate and disagreement occurred in the previous chapter with the process theologian Hartshorne and Hopper, a modern theologian and their viewpoints of the New Testament canon.

1. Hopper, *Modern Theology II*, 85.

This inability for consensus from within concerning the issue of authority demonstrates the difficulty of holding sand in your hands. Try as you might the sand slips through your fingers. In a similar way, try as they might to create a new authority, it continues to slip away. Authority becomes whoever shouts the loudest or longest. Or whoever can gather the most votes. Or something that can only be truly known within the self since language itself can become a form of manipulation and oppression and only the self knows the actual meaning and purpose of a word as it is being used.

A brief discussion on the use of language is needed. Most people understand that a word can have multiple meanings. One example is the word "cool." With an understanding of the context and the tone of one's voice the meaning of the word "cool" can be understood within a group.

Within the liberal voices of the Christian choir, the meaning of words can change. We have already seen how the words "liberal" and "conservative" can change within context and audience. This also occurs with the word equality. Is it being used within a cultural or biblical framework? It seems to be occurring with the phrase "Do No Harm." It occurs all the time with discussions on fairness.

The manipulation of language can be a very effective entry point for the *re-education* of the conservative or traditional Christian from the point of view of the modern process theologian. It is hard to argue that fairness is not an important idea. In this way, a cultural understanding of fairness might seem harmless to one's biblical foundations, except when one considers how unfair God's grace is! Grace and fairness are not the same thing. For no one deserves God's grace. It is not fair from a worldly standpoint for God to pour out grace upon us all. It is rather an undeserved act of love.

Today we hear arguments about fairness, sexuality, and even the concept of marriage. Hopper writes the following concerning sexuality,

> Increasingly today Christian theologians judge that the witness of Scripture (and tradition) to the love of God for all creatures is incompatible with both sexual limited

conceptions of God and sexist social structures. Both can seem dehumanizing in their effects, and thus contrary to the grace of God which we have learned through those historically and culturally human witnesses to the embodiment of God-for-us in Jesus Christ.[2]

Notice that Hopper is no longer using Scripture (the Bible) or tradition to be authoritative in matters of sexuality and "sexist social structures." In this way, when discussing fairness, sexuality, and marriage, one must first discuss what one is using as authoritative. I am amazed how many people I have met (even pastor colleagues) who have no idea that the homosexual/lesbian marriage by the Christian church has nothing to do with fairness (however that word might be used at the time) and everything to do with biblical and traditional concepts of authority.

Finally, it is with a great deal of frustration that I write that within this debate, the homosexual and lesbian communities are being *used* and directed away from free, universal, responsible grace of Jesus into a works type of living. This is tragic! I have talked with people who have told me that they cannot be Christian because they are gay. How sad and untrue! Jesus is the Savior of the world and is for all. John 4:42 reads, "They said to the woman, 'It is no longer because of what you have said that we believe, for we have heard for ourselves, and we know that this is truly the Savior of the world.'"

I always answer this misinformed comment on gay issues the same way. I invite the person to read the gospels of Jesus Christ found in the Bible. Read either Matthew, Mark, Luke or John. Or if you get really ambitious, read all four. Then come back and we will discuss together all the times homosexuality or lesbians are discussed within these gospels

I know the answer. There is none. However, grace and new life and forgiveness and repentance and healing and renewal are found all the time.

Clearly, the Christian does not exclude the homosexual/lesbian communities. All are welcome through the same gifts of free,

---

2. Hopper, *Modern Theology II*, 95.

universal, responsible grace. Obviously this allows room for much discussion and debate within the Christian choir and at the same time it does not jettison Jesus, access to a personal relationship with God through Christ, the cross and the universal gift of free grace.

QUESTIONS FOR REVIEW REFLECTION, AND DISCUSSION

1. What is the paradox of authority and freedom?
2. What is the result of modern theology's struggle to hold onto the paradox of authority and freedom?
3. Why is fairness a different starting point than what is found as a biblical starting point?
4. The author discusses the woman about to be stoned and the new life found in Christ that she knows through Jesus's free, universal, responsible grace. Have you ever experienced this reality within the Christian faith or know someone who has? Discuss if desired.

Truth a Foundation for Peace

Speaking the truth in love
Ephesians 4:15a

Truth is a foundational block for personal peace. Alcoholic Anonymous groups are built upon this foundation. Healing for the alcoholic begins when they are able to state the truth, "My name is . . . and I am an alcoholic." When this truth is stated a new journey and a new life can begin.

Grief support groups are built on this same foundation of truth, the truth moving from denial to the truth that a loved one has died. Truth then moves the person from anger to sadness and loss and eventually comfort and the gift of faith, to "peace that passes understanding" (Phil. 4:7).

Earlier, I talked about the importance of truth in the healing of a person with post-traumatic stress disorder, where the ability to name the lie then leads to new opportunities for renewal and healing and life. Persons with post-abortion syndrome, (or whatever anxiety issue a person chooses to use), find the point of healing in truth in a very similar way. For many, healing begins with a statement of truth which occurs by naming the fetus/unborn child. This naming can allow a person to then move into more natural and open forms of grief.

Without this truth a person can feel stuck in stages of denial and/or anger (sometimes misplaced anger) and prolonged sadness. This occurs when a person has been convinced of an untruth, when a person is told that an abortion is an end or that they should not talk about this with family and friends. These are untruths that stunt healing and peace. Abortion in truth is a difficult decision among many difficult decisions. And the result—despite whatever choice is made—will be a difficult one with lasting effects. Further, repressing feelings and creating a fantasy world by not talking with family and friends is not helpful. A person needs to tell their story regardless of their beliefs concerning abortion. Further, a support system of family and friends can be a gift and a true source of healing.

Finally, it is not uncommon for persons within modern and process perspectives to struggle with special needs persons and persons with very limited intellectual capabilities. This is not said as a put down. It is simply a statement of truth.

In the chapter "Abortion and Truth," I discussed the importance of fluent speech and reasoning, in Hartshorne's perspective, that were vitally important in determining those who are quite certainly persons.[1]

This is not to say that persons from modernist or process perspectives do not like special needs people. But rather, what it is saying is that within their perspectives there is a built in difficulty since human reason has been elevated above divine inspiration and in many cases the idea of divine inspiration has been long ago discarded as the meditations of a pre-modern or primitive mind.

This is a very different starting point than that of biblical authority, universal grace, tradition, and the witness of the faithful throughout the ages. Just think of the impact two Christian women, one named Anne Sullivan and the other Helen Keller, made on the world and the dignity found in all persons.

As a young girl, Helen Keller became both blind and unable to hear. Anne Sullivan relied on her creativity, intellect and a stubborn faith concerning the human spirit to teach Helen language. First, a simple form of letter-writing in a person's hand and later the ability to make vocal sounds by touching and mimicking the

---

1. Hartshorne, *Omnipotence*, 102.

voice vibrations of a person speaking. Eventually, with the constant aid of Anne Sullivan, Helen attended and graduated from Harvard and traveled the world as an international spokesperson. Anne Sullivan and Helen Keller changed the way the world perceives and seeks to treat persons with special needs.

I remember a religion class I had in middle school. I went to a Christian school and during the class, we were asked the question, "Is a child unable to speak as valuable as Albert Einstein?" From a worldly standpoint this is an absurd question. Obviously, Albert Einstein is more valuable. Just think of all the contributions he made to our understanding of mathematics and physics and to the world. From a biblical standpoint of faith, the question is equally absurd. Obviously the child (who one day will grow into an adult) is of equal value as Albert Einstein. Through the journey of faith, we are invited to figure out why.

Parents of special needs children know the importance of grieving the child that was dreamed of within one's mind and heart to then be able to celebrate the child that is. The article *Special Kids, Extraordinary Parents* beautifully describes this healing that is based on the foundation of truth. The truth is every potential parent has a secret dream of the child that will be. We dream of kicking a ball or playing dress up, of school days or graduation ceremonies or weddings of grandchildren. All parents do these kinds of dreams, but then encounter the reality, the truth that this will not be the life that their newborn will have. These dreams will have to die and a parent will need to grieve. This will then allow new life and new dreams to develop. It will allow the parent to love and celebrate the child that is in truth.

The writer, teacher, and theologian Henri Nouwen gives a beautiful account of his learning to understand "Adam speech." In the book *Adam: God's Beloved*, Nouwen talks about the utter terror when first assigned to care for Adam and to get Adam dressed for the day. Adam was a man who could not speak or even move without assistance. He also had frequent seizures. Later, Nouwen talks about developing "Adam's eyes" and the love he had for Adam. He even calls Adam the best spiritual director he ever had.[2]

Nouwen wrote these words after Adam died, which speak of the dignity and blessedness that Nouwen had come to know because of the gift of Adam.

> From the moment I saw Adam's body lying in the casket, I was struck by the mystery of this man's life and death. In a flash I knew in my heart that this disabled human being was loved by God from all eternity and sent him into the world with a unique mission of healing, which was now fulfilled.
>
> I recognized many parallels between the story of Jesus and the story of Adam. And I knew something else. I knew, in a very profound place, that Adam in some mysterious way, had become an image of the living Christ for me just as Jesus, when he lived on the earth, was a friend, teacher, and guide for his disciples. In and through Adam, I came to a truly new understanding of those relationships of Jesus, not just as they were lived long ago, but as Jesus desires to live them now, with me and with us, through the weakest and most vulnerable people. Indeed, not only did I come to know more about God by caring for Adam, but Adam helped me, by his life, to discover and rediscover the Spirit of Jesus alive in our own "poorness of spirit." Jesus lived long ago, but Adam lived in my time. Jesus was physically present to his disciples. Adam was physically present to me. Jesus was Emmanuel, God with us. Adam became for me a sacred person, a holy man, an image of the living God.
>
> Was Adam very unusual? Was he some special angel? Not at all. Adam was one person among many others. But I had a relationship with Adam, and he became special for me. I loved him, and our relationship was one of the most significant of my life. Adam's death touched me deeply because for me he was the one who more than any professor or book led me to the person of Jesus. His

2. Nouwen, *Adam*, 34.

death was a wake-up call. It seemed as if he said to me, "Now that I have left you, you can write about me and tell your friends and readers what I have taught you about the mystery of our wonderful God who came to dwell among us and who sent us the Holy Spirit."[3]

Later, Nouwen wrote about Adam's parents and their journey to accept and celebrate the Adam that was.

> For Adam, God was never the subject of an intellectual or emotional speech. Like Jesus, his belovedness, his likeness to God, his mission of peace could be acknowledged only by those willing to welcome him as one sent by God.
>
> Most people saw Adam as a disabled person, who had little to give and who was a burden to his family, his community, and to society at large. And as long as he was seen in this way, his truth was hidden. What was not received was not given.
>
> But Adam's parents loved him simply because he was Adam. Yes, they recognized and loved him for himself. Without awareness they also welcomed him as one sent to us by God in utter vulnerability to be an instrument of God's blessing. That vision of him changes everything quite radically because then Adam emerges as someone, as special, as a wonderful gift, child of promise.[4]

The apostle Paul wrote many years ago,

> For the message about the cross is foolishness to those who are perishing, but to us who are being saved it is the power of God. For it is written, 'I will destroy the wisdom of the wise, and the discernment of the discerning I will thwart.' Where is the one who is wise? Where is the scribe? Where is the debater of his age? Has not God made foolish the wisdom of the world? For since, the wisdom of God, the world did not know God through wisdom, God decided through the foolishness of our

---

3. Nouwen, *Adam*, 15–16.
4. Nouwen, *Adam*, 30–31.

proclamation, to those who believe. For Jews demand signs and Greeks desire wisdom, but we proclaim Christ crucified, a stumbling block to Jews and foolishness to Gentiles, but to those who are called, both Jews and Greeks, Christ the power of God and the wisdom of God. For God's foolishness is wiser than human wisdom, and God's weakness is stronger than human strength. (1 Cor 1:18–25).

It is to the cross that I will return in the final chapter, "Trapped in Works and the Rediscovery of Free Grace." But first, let us examine "Truth as a Foundation for Peace" within a larger scale, among communities, religions, and throughout the world. Cardinal Francis Arinze talks about this need for truth as a basis for peace within world affairs. In his book *Religions for Peace: A Call for Solidarity to the Religions of the World*, Arinze writes,

> God is the creator of all humanity. In following his will, inserted into human nature guided by right reason, is the peace of all men and women.
>
> Human life is sacred. It must be protected. We have no right to kill ourselves or to kill innocent people. While self-defense is a right and is justifiable, it has to be kept with due limits.
>
> Justice, peace, tranquility in the world are built on the respect for the fundamental rights of other people, especially their right to life, religious freedom, and free exercise of political, economic, and cultural rights. Economic and political development of peoples is also an obligatory road to peace. If people are illiterate, underdeveloped, oppressed, and repressed, the justice and peace are rendered more difficult.
>
> Violence, terrorism, the taking of human lives, and the destruction of property are condemned by all genuine religions. They are opposed to love of God and neighbor. No matter the problems and challenges to be faced, these violent roads are the wrong ones. Solutions in line with respect for God and humanity have to be sought,

no matter how difficult and long-termed they may be. All religions are bound to help their followers engage in reflections such as these.[5]

QUESTIONS FOR REVIEW REFLECTION, AND DISCUSSION

1. Why is it that modernist and process perspectives struggle with special needs persons and with persons with very limited intellectual abilities?

2. What are the names of special needs persons you have known? How have they contributed to your life?

---

5. Arinze, *Religions for Peace*, vii–viii.

Trapped in Works and the Rediscovery of Free Grace

For there is no distinction since all have sinned and fall short of the glory of God; they are now justified by his grace as a gift through redemption that is in Jesus Christ.

ROMANS 3:22B-24

THROUGHOUT THIS BOOK, I have been highlighting the differences that occur within some of the more liberal or modernist or process oriented or progressive voices within the Christian choir from those found in Bible believing or conservative or orthodox or classical or evangelical or fundamentalist voices within the Christian choir. These differences are natural outcomes since inclusion is a much smaller vision than universality. It occurs with the de-emphasis of the canonical Gospels. This leads to the need for a new Gnosticism which eventually leads to a new works mentality and a very small group of new enlightened. It occurs with the loss of authority of canonical scripture, and the de-emphasis of tradition and the witness of the faithful throughout the ages which results in the creation of relative grace. This relative grace is ultimately governed by the self and in practice looks an awful lot like cheap grace.

In his book *God: The Evidence*, Patrick Glynn describes his movement from faith to agnosticism and then to atheism. In this type of viewpoint, even though one no longer believes that a living, loving creative God really exists, the idea of church and faith remains since it provides opportunities for community, group charity work, and a nice psychological crutch, that—when kept in balance—can be somewhat helpful to the individual. Glynn writes about this journey,

> For despite the fact that the overwhelming majority of Americans are believers, our intellectual culture has been dominated by skepticism. When I did undergraduate work at Harvard in the 1970s for example, it was taken for granted that traditional religious beliefs were a thing of the past, invalidated by science, incompatible with modern outlook. There were believers among the professors, of course. But the culture was agnostic. There was a tendency, which I came to share, to view religious beliefs and practices as manifestations of intellectual inconsistency, emotional weakness, or lack of cultural sophistication.[1]

Later Glynn writes,

> It was not so much that the professors who taught me were anti-religious—the English department faculty (apart from a couple of practicing Catholics and a few other churchgoers) were marked by a sad yearning for lost Christianity. It was simply assumed that religious belief had become impossible for rational human beings in the modern era, a fact that once accepted with a certain melancholy and nostalgia for previous ages when it was possible for "men" to believe. Some thought, following the nineteenth-century writer Matthew Arnold, that with religion gone, literature, would somehow have to take its place. But that was a halfhearted notion.
>
> Such views reflected the confidence of the intellectual world that modern science had destroyed all rational foundation for the religious worldview. "We moderns" were the heirs of the two great scientific revolutions: Copernican and Darwinian.[2]

---

1. Glynn, *God*, 1–2.
2. Glynn, *God*, 4.

Glynn concludes this journey.

> By the time I received my PhD at the end of the 1970s, I was a convinced atheist. The embrace of atheism did not bring joy. Somehow, despite my "agnosticism" I had clung to the hope that I might be proven wrong. The day I grasped that the entire tradition of Western philosophy, from ancient to modern times, was essentially a refutation of the religious worldview—of the idea of God—was not a happy one. But the conclusion seemed inescapable. Reason, I thought was the only path to truth.[3]

Eventually, Glynn returned to faith and his journey back to God chronicled throughout his book is both fascinating and inspiring. With his return to faith, Glynn also experiences a return to meaning and renewed joy.

The Christian working with a biblical, traditional understanding of Jesus's grace is always "free"! Grace is never "cheap." Matthew 10:8 reads, "Freely you have received, now freely give."

This rediscovery of free grace results, once again, by re-examining Jesus and the cross. The cross of Christ is not only a sign of victory and resurrection but also a sign of agony and death. It is this cross that Jesus willingly hung upon for the salvation of you and me and to draw *all* persons to himself (John 12:32). It is through maintaining and meditating on the reality of the cross that we do not drift into the temptation of cheap grace and stay rooted in the gift of free grace.

In the chapter "The Quest for Christ and the Reality of Jesus," I examined a conversation Lee Strobel had with Professor Edwin M. Yamauchi. Yamauchi, using credible evidence of Jesus outside of the biographies of Jesus, concluded with an astounding summary of evidence.[4] Briefly summarizing these findings, it is concluded that a man named Jesus lived in a certain area at a certain time in history, and that he was hung upon and died on a cross is not debatable. What it means and how God worked and continues

---

3. Glynn, *God*, 5.
4. Strobel, *Case for Christ*, 87.

to work through the cross of Christ is worthy of reflection and contemplation.

That followers of this Jesus would claim that he rose from the grave is a fact of history. That future, followers of this Jesus continue to talk about the resurrection and new life known in Christ is a living reality.

Dietrich Bonhoeffer's writings on the cross of Christ are especially helpful and it continues to be through a mature understanding of the cross that free, universal, responsible grace becomes alive for many persons who choose to follow Jesus. In this light, I was drawn once again to his book titled *Meditations on the Cross* and a poem Bonhoeffer wrote from the Tegel prison in 1944.

Bonhoeffer was a German Lutheran pastor who argued against Hitler and the tendencies he saw within the Nazi regime. He had already lived for two years in a concentration camp at the time that he wrote this poem, part of a longer personal letter, and he would know his earthly death by hanging the following year. Bonhoeffer's witness and willingness to stay in Germany (though he had been encouraged to escape in earlier years) to minister to God's people and to seek a reformation in his country continues to speak. Bonhoeffer wrote,

> Christians and Pagans
>
> 1. People go to God in their need,
> for help, happiness and bread they plead
> for deliverance from sickness, guilt and
> death. Thus do they all, Christians and
> pagans.
>
> 2. People go to God in God's need,
> find God poor, reviled, with neither
> shelter nor bread, see God entangled in
> sin, weakness and death. Christians
> stand by God in God's suffering.
>
> 3. God comes to all human beings in need,
> satisfies them body and soul with His

> bread, dies the death of the cross for
> Christians and pagans, and forgives them
> both.[5]

The discovery, or rediscovery, of free grace through the cross of Christ allows us to understand the things that make us limp in a spiritual sense. The truth is life is not always easy, the journey of life is full of joys and pain, celebrations and scars and every person in some way limps. Joseph Girzone says it this way in his book *A Portrait of Jesus*,

> Jesus' love is not superficial or fickle. Friendship doesn't end just because we do stupid things, especially out of our weakness. It's all right! All Jesus' friends limp or are seriously defective in some way. It doesn't bother Him. That is what is so extraordinary about God's love.[6]

A biblical foundation and personal relationship with Jesus provides the foundation for a new and abundant life. John 10:10b reads, "I came that you might have life and have it abundantly." It is this new life in Christ, this gospel—this good news to all-that I am called to preach.

QUESTIONS FOR REVIEW REFLECTION, AND DISCUSSION

1. Why is works living a natural outcome within much of modern liberal thought and how can a rediscovery of free grace lead to new life?

---

5. Bonhoeffer, *Meditations on the Cross*, 60.
6. Girzone, *Portrait of Jesus*, 28–29.

PART TWO

The Conversation Continues

Fall 2022

Jesus is the same yesterday and today and forever.
HEBREWS 13:8

IT'S ALL BACKWARDS!

On May 1, 2022, the United Methodist Church birthed a new denomination called the Global Methodist Church. Why did the orthodox/conservative/evangelical voice within the church choose to depart the United Methodist Church? Why was it not the liberal/postmodern/progressive voice within the church to depart from the United Methodist Church?

On February 26, 2019, a National Public Radio article announced "United Methodist Church Votes to Keep Bans on Same-Sex Weddings, LGBTQ Clergy." The article reported that the General Conference delegates from around the world voted 438 to 384 in favor of the traditional plan, thus maintaining the United Methodist Church teaching and doctrine on these issues.[1]

This begs the question, why was it then the orthodox/conservative/evangelical voice within the church that chose to depart the United Methodist Church? As mentioned earlier, this group would later birth the Global Methodist Church.

---

1. Chappell, "Votes to Keep Bans."

Do You Still Believe in Miracles?

The answer is theology and potential ramifications that can naturally flow from theology. To move the conversation forward, we must briefly look back to recent history to then develop a framework for understanding current events.

Throughout my entire ministry as a United Methodist pastor (1995-present) I believed the United Methodist Church would split. It has been clear that the church in the United States has been declining in membership while the United Methodist Church internationally was growing rapidly. Further, it was apparent that many areas of church growth, including Africa and the Philippines, primarily resided in the orthodox/conservative/evangelical voice within the church. These communities often expressed traditional understandings of Christian marriage.

In this light, it was obvious that the liberal/postmodern/progressive voice within the United Methodist Church would never get enough votes to change the teaching of the church concerning marriage. It was reasonable to think that every four years at General Conference, the gap between those favoring marriage in traditional terms and those advocating for the LGBTQ+ community and gay marriage would widen.

Logic would believe that, faced with this reality, there would be a bishop or bishops who resided in the liberal/postmodern/progressive voice of the United Methodist Church who would lead like-minded Christian believers out of the United Methodist Church. As a local pastor, I believed I was called to care for those within the local church during a time of change and loss. Further, it was my hope and prayer that the birthing of a new denomination that felt called to serve the LGBTQ+ community, a community previously underserved, would be done in a gracious and celebratory way.

This gracious and celebratory action did not happen. So, we must return to the question "Why?" and explore the answer, "Theology."

QUESTIONS FOR REVIEW, REFLECTION, AND DISCUSSION

1. What was the final vote count of the United Methodist General Conference held in February 2019?
2. What was the traditional plan?
3. What is the name of the denomination birthed on May 1, 2022? What branch of the United Methodist Church did this new Wesleyan denomination represent?

Paternalistic Tendencies in Progressive Theology

So the last will be first, and the first will be last.
MATTHEW 19:30

IT IS SAID THAT a picture paints a thousand words. I was ordained an Elder in the Wisconsin Conference in the United Methodist Church in the summer of 1999. This poster was by the entrance to the Wisconsin Annual Conference 2019. I took a picture of the poster on June 14, 2019.

PATERNALISTIC TENDENCIES IN PROGRESSIVE THEOLOGY

For twenty years, I worked with respected colleagues and co-workers in Christ as a member of the Wisconsin Conference. I believed that is how we saw each other: respected colleagues and co-workers in Christ. Entering the conference in June 2019, I realized that was no longer the case. Somehow, those who disagreed with each other were enemies. In other words, a dividing line had been created and one must choose on what side of the line you stood.

I realized that I had friends and co-workers who would be on different sides of the line. I wondered where people would place me on the line. I realized that schism within the church was inevitable, though I had no idea how that schism would occur.

What is in a name? A lot can be learned by a name. In the Roman Catholic church, the concept of the universal message of Jesus is so important it is in the name: "catholic," meaning "universal" in Latin. Within the Lutheran church, the teachings of Luther and his understanding of salvation by grace and faith are prominent. Within the Pentecostal church, drawing upon Pentecost, the living activity of the Holy Spirit is emphasized. Within a Methodist church, there is an emphasis of teaching laity methods and tools to grow in their personal relationship with Jesus and then empowering people to put their faith into action in their daily lives.

A lot can be learned by a name. The term "progressive church" assumes a state of enlightenment. The definition of progressive is "happening or developing gradually or in stages."[1] A problem can occur if a community believes that they have somehow "progressed" beyond or above other communities. When this occurs, division is inevitable.

In 1 Cor chapter 12, the apostle Paul addresses the conflict within the church of Corinth. Some members had received the gift of speaking in tongues. A problem within the church occurred when some began to rate the ways fellow believers experienced God. Some even implied that to be a real Christian, one must speak in tongues. In other words, a dividing line had been created within the church at Corinth.

---

1. *Pocket Oxford American Dictionary*, 654.

Paul does not deny the validity of their gift. At the same time, Paul utilizes the image of the body of Christ to then illustrate a different way of seeing unity and the various gifts God might bestow on the community.

Many times, Jesus addresses the human tendency to rate each other. Jesus teaches, "So the last will be first, and the first will be last" (Matt 20:16). On another occasion, when asked by his disciples, "Who is the greatest in the kingdom of heaven" (Matt 18:1), Jesus called a little child to him and taught those around him to "change and become like little children" (Matt 18:3), thus challenging the norms of society based on conventional ways of rating each other, one over or better than another.

St. John of the Cross spoke into this new vision of being with each other.

> When our hearts are free from liking and judging people merely according to their natural gifts, we are not held captive by external and changing charms. We are instead free to love people as they are, and we can penetrate more easily to the core of their personality, their true goodness.[2]

My scriptural home is a symphonic approach to Johannine literature, meaning the Gospel of John, and the letters of 1 John, 2 John and 3 John. In studying these passages, I have found great insight from thinkers James McPolin[3] and Donald Senior.[4] In this regard, I seek grace and truth (John 1:17b) to be the lens by which I perceive reality. Everyone has a lens by which they perceive reality. For me, grace means I need to provide grace to others and myself; truth means that there is healing and freedom that can be known in truth.

In this light, I need to address the issue of cultural colonialism with my respected colleagues and co-workers in Christ who find their home within progressive theologies. Honest dialogue benefits all, many times revealing blind spots that we all have and paths that, when illuminated, we may not want to repeat.

---

2. Ruth, *Daily Readings*, 40.
3. McPolin, *John*.
4. Senior, *Passion of Jesus*.

A definition of colonialism reads, "the practice of acquiring control over another country."[5] In everyday living, it meant that the person in power never recognizes the person dependent or below themselves as an equal. Colonialism can be an extreme outcome of paternalism.

The most recent United Methodist Church General Conference occurred April 23 through May 3, 2024. During this General Conference, delegates passed a resolution to end anti-LGBTQ church laws. This vote passed after more than 7600 mostly conservative congregations chose to disaffiliate from the United Methodist Church.[6] The 2024 General Conference was different from previous conferences as a result of these disaffiliations. It is reasonable to deduce that the change of the composition of voting delegates had an impact on the resolution to end anti-LGBTQ church laws.

Unfortunately, for some within the African community, the logistics of the conference provided echoes of a colonial time where African ideas and full participation were marginalized and dismissed. In an open letter before the 2024 General Conference, the United Methodist Africa Forum (UMAF) voiced concerns that several unresolved issues would produce "limitations to meaningful and effective participation of the African church at the upcoming General Conference."[7]

The article, Message from African Delegation at 2024 General Conference, posted on May 2, 2024, written after the historic vote that changed the United Methodist position on LGBTQ issues, expressed continued frustrations experienced by the African delegation. The article begins,

> We speak as Africans, representing the majority of African delegates and, we believe the vast majority of United Methodists in the thirty-five annual conferences in Africa.[8]

---

5. *Pocket Oxford Dictionary*, 150.
6. Maddox, "United Methodist Church."
7. United Methodist Africa Forum, "Open Letter."
8. Good News, "Message from African Delegates."

Later they write,

> Many African delegates are not here. They desired to be present and had planned to attend. But they were not invited by the Commission on General Conference in time to receive their visas. Over 70 of us from Africa are not present. That is roughly 25% of our delegates. Ten months ago we began sending letters and emails and making phone calls, alerting the Commission on General Conference and some bishops that there was a problem. Many of these communications never received a single response. It felt as if we were not valued or wanted.[9]

This message was signed by Rev. Dr. Jerry Kulah, Head of Delegation, Liberia Conference; Mr. Prosperous Tunda, Delegate, East Congo Annual Conference; Rev. Dr. Danjuma Judi, Nigeria Annual Conference; Dr. Yeabu Kamara, Delegate, Sierra Leone Annual Conference; and Mr. Ginford Dzimati, Delegate, Zimbabwe Annual Conference.[10] The point is not to discuss and debate the results of the votes taken at the 2024 General Conference. The point is to question why so many from the African community voiced concerns and were not heard and were ultimately dismissed.

The question I am raising is the possibility that progressive theology makes it more difficult to hear the concerns and wisdom of communities that have previously been treated in paternalistic ways. It may also make it more possible to repeat a different form of colonialism called cultural colonialism. I believe this is what many in the African church are trying to reveal, and the question remains, "Why are they not being heard?"

---

9. Message from African Delegates at 2024 General Conference, Good News Magazine.

10. Message from African Delegates at 2024 General Conference, Good News Magazine.

QUESTIONS FOR REVIEW, REFLECTION, AND DISCUSSION

1. What is the definition of "progressive?"
2. What occurred as a result of the historic vote taken on May 2, 2024, at the General Conference of the United Methodist Church?
3. What is the definition of cultural colonialism?

A Conversation with a United Methodist Bishop

Now if Christ is proclaimed as raised from the dead, how can some of you say there is no resurrection of the dead?

If there is no resurrection of the dead, then Christ has not been raised; and if Christ has not been raised, then our proclamation has been in vain and your faith has been in vain.

1 Corinthians 15:12–14

In this chapter, I am going to dialogue with C. Joseph Sprague. Sprague began his theological education at the Methodist Theological School in Ohio (MTSO) in 1965. I began my education at MTSO in 1993. Sprague became a bishop in the United Methodist Church in 1996. He served in the Chicago Episcopal Area and the Northern Illinois Conference from 1996 to 2004.

My intent is to dialogue with Sprague's book *Affirmation of a Dissenter*, published in 2002. I will first provide an honest uplifting of his theology and the potential positive aspects it could play in the broader Christian choir. Second, I will critique Sprague's argument from a orthodox perspective. Third, I will highlight predictable outcomes from Sprague's thesis.

Sprague writes, "The longer I live—and I am now Social Security eligible—the stronger grows my trust in and commitment to God's hospitable and unconditional love."[1] Later, he continues by addressing his audience,

> I write especially for those on the way who need kindred voices, honest minds, welcoming hearts, and the gift of candor to "keep on keeping on" in a church that often talks about Jesus, but fails to be the institutional expression of the One whose hospitality was inclusive and universal.[2]

Sprague affirms Jesus as Liberator and Savior.[3] When speaking on the Bible, Sprague writes,

> I do strongly affirm that the Bible is and ever shall be the primary source of authority for all Christians and that biblical authority must not be viewed as static truth that falls off the pages of the Bible. Instead, it is a dynamic process that is empowered by the work of the Holy Spirit in the midst of the faith community's discernment process through prayer, dialogue, informed scholarship, and application to the issues of today.[4]

Sprague aligns himself with progressive theology writing,

> Progressives believe that from Genesis to Revelation, the trajectory of the biblical witness is God's inclusive love that calls all humankind into covenant with the Holy One through the hospitable and God-manifesting witness and life of the people of the Covenant, namely, Israel and the church.[5]

Sprague invites us to recognize the outcast and those not currently having their needs met by traditional forms of church. Sprague champions the rights of the LGBTQ community.

> The homosexuality controversy has not been for me the troubling issue it has been for many Christians. From a

---

1. Sprague, *Affirmation of a Dissenter*, 7.
2. Sprague, *Affirmation of a Dissenter*, 7.
3. Sprague, *Affirmation of a Dissenter*, 8.
4. Sprague, *Affirmation of a Dissenter*, 22.
5. Sprague, *Affirmation of a Dissenter*, 21.

biblical and theological point of view, I understand gay and lesbian persons to be victims, like yesterday's lepers and today's people of color, who have been adjudged to be outsiders by the rigid, exclusive mandates of church attitudes and/or laws.[6]

Later Sprague writes,

> A key question that the church must address is not one of sexual orientation any more than race or gender. Variables of sexual orientation, color, and gender are inherent givens. Christ has broken down all dividing walls of hostility. We have been made One in baptism; therefore, the question for the Church is not one of inherent givens, but how the Church can support people, as they were created by God, as they seek in faith to make the journey of discipleship toward wholeness.[7]

AN ORTHODOX CRITIQUE OF SPRAGUE

Sprague frames his argument in dualistic terms which is different from Trinitarian terms. As a result, he seeks to proclaim God as a soloist, thus needing conformity, rather than a choir which seeks authenticity. Irwyn L. Ince Jr. in his book *The Beautiful Community: Unity, Diversity, and the Church at its Best* writes from a Trinitarian perspective,

> For humanity to be the image of God, it must embody beautiful community—unity in diversity, diversity in unity. If God displays his beauty in his Trinitarian life, we should expect that beauty to be reflected in the humanity that images him. While each person is royalty, we find the fullest expression of the image in community.[8]

---

6. Sprague, *Affirmation of a Dissenter*, 96.
7. Sprague, *Affirmation of a Dissenter*, 101.
8. Ince, *Beautiful Community*, 55.

A CONVERSATION WITH A UNITED METHODIST BISHOP

Sprague writes, "I hereby dissent from the arrogance of neoliteralism."[9] Earlier, he spoke of the "idolatry of biblical literalism."[10] It is difficult to understand how honest discourse and discussion can be found with one whose arguments you are labeling arrogant and idolatrous.

Sprague writes,

> I affirm the Bible as the primary means whereby God reveals both immanence and transcendence and calls the church and each of us into relationship with the God revealed in Jesus. The primacy of scripture is certain. How we approach this treasure is crucial. I believe that neoliteralism is theologically inconsistent and hurtful to the long term faithfulness and viability of the whole church. I appeal to progressives to advocate for their understanding of biblical authority in order that the Bible might be rescued from neoliteralism for the benefit of the whole church.[11]

What does Sprague mean by neoliteralism? First, is the reality of the virgin birth. Sprague rejects the reality of the virgin birth and affirms that "the theological myth of the virgin birth points to this wondrous and ultimate truth."[12] Second, Sprague denies the literal resurrection of Jesus. Sprague writes, "I believe in the resurrection of Jesus, but I cannot affirm that his resurrection involved the resuscitation of his physical body."[13]

As an orthodox Christian, I do believe in the virgin birth and the actual resurrection of Jesus from the grave. This is consistent with the apostolic witness and the testimony of the Christian faithful. Does that mean I am an idolatrous and arrogant neoliteralist? A neoliteralist from whom others need to be rescued?

Again, Sprague has framed his argument in a us/them dynamic that does not foster dialogue. This is different from unity

---

9. Sprague, *Affirmation of a Dissenter*, 22.
10. Sprague, *Affirmation of a Dissenter*, 17.
11. Sprague, *Affirmation of a Dissenter*, 35.
12. Sprague, *Affirmation of a Dissenter*, 40.
13. Sprague, *Affirmation of a Dissenter*, 41.

within diversity and diversity within unity which is a characteristic of Trinitarian theology and the potential for harmony among those who think and believe differently.

As a student at MTSO (1993–1996), it became clear to me that the teaching of those like Sprague, who denied the virgin birth and the actual resurrection of Jesus, could not get to a love ethic to all. Instead of a love ethic to all, there was simply a substitution of who was in the in-group and who was in the out-group. Instead of a call for growth and authenticity, there was a push for conformity, since to do otherwise could be considered primitive-minded, silly and, in some cases, evil. Second, was the realization the denial of the physical resurrection of Jesus would inevitably lead to the loss of free, universal, responsible grace.

It is not surprising that Sprague redefines the atonement and the need for the atonement. Sprague writes,

> I affirm Jesus, the fully human one, as the Son of God, whose relationship of faithful trust and radical obedience with God gave to the church (and through the church to the world) the preeminent manifestation of at-one-ment with God. Atonement is the English contraction for at-one-ment. Obviously, such an understanding of atonement leaves no room to affirm substitutionary atonement theory that portrays Jesus' blood on the cross as satisfying an angry deity through one majestic sacrificial human death, much as sacrifices of unblemished sheep and goats in ancient Israel were understood to appease God and atone for the sins of all.[14]

PREDICTABLE OUTCOMES FROM SPRAGUE'S THESIS

It is possible that the United Methodist Church can become a home to the LGBTQ+ community and those who do not have their needs met by traditional forms of church. It is also predictable that those currently in leadership would deem it virtuous to not abide

14. Sprague, *Affirmation of a Dissenter*, 7.

by the will of the collective church, since a progressive theology is assuming a position of supremacy over other points of view. It is also predictable along a similar line of thinking to disregard the collective wisdom of the international community in a way that demonstrates a lack of self-awareness to cultural colonialism. This occurs even when those who have been colonized declare they are being colonized again and the wisdom within their communities is once again being minimized and discarded.

Finally, the effort to confine God into human terms of a soloist does not allow Sprague and those he represents to dialogue with other voices within the Christian choir. As a result, it is possible to become what you started out seeking to refute. Sprague writes concerning the purpose of his book,

> This offering is for all who affirm Jesus as Liberator and Savior, but who are vexed in the deepest recesses of their souls with the attempted takeover of the church by closed minds and fearful hearts, which seek security in rigid literalism, narrow parochialism, and hurtful exclusivism.[15]

Could this not be a description of the current UMC leadership? As stated earlier the church universal voted at the 2019 General Conference 438 to 384 to maintain a traditional understanding of Christian marriage and LGBTQ+ clergy. One can argue that the progressive branch of the church demonstrated a coup by not adhering to the will of the people. Second, the decision to regionalize the church[16] reinforces the position of those claiming cultural colonialism and the rejection of the collective wisdom known in various places in the world that then build up the Christian choir, the family of God. Third, the rejection of neoliteralism and those who believe in this way becomes its own form of literalism and subsequent exclusivism. It is exclusivism because only like-minded people are included and have progressed to a certain place of enlightenment. Is not cancel culture, shouting down those

---

15. Sprague, *Affirmation of a Dissenter*, 7.
16. Hahn et al., "General Conference Gives Regionalization."

who have different viewpoints and ghosting people, a form of exclusivism? "Ghosting" is defined as "the act or practice of abruptly cutting off all contact with someone usually without explanation by no longer responding to phone calls, instant messages, etc."[17] Fourth, without grace, we are limited to human understandings of power and the human imagination.

This again, is very different from Christian communities based on grace, authenticity, and unity within diversity and diversity within unity. Jesus frees us from the confines of the human imagination. Jesus redefines our understanding of power through the cross and resurrection. The Trinity continues to redefine our understanding of power, thus creating freedom for a variety of faithful expressions in harmony to a common dignity known in our createdness and the cornerstone of Christ (Eph 2:19–22). Finally, the virgin birth informs us that we are not alone and God in God's love has come to dwell among us. Matthew 1:23 states, "'Look, the virgin shall conceive and bear a son, and they shall name him Emmanuel,' which means, 'God is with us.'" The truth of the bodily resurrection of Jesus reminds us that God has chosen to be with us always. Therefore, the apostle Peter is able to proclaim that hope is not limited to a human emotion but rather is rooted in a living relationship with the risen Lord. 1 Peter 1:3 reads, "Blessed be the God and Father of our Lord Jesus Christ! By his great mercy he has given us a new birth into a living hope through the resurrection of Jesus Christ from the dead."

It is my belief that dialogue within the various branches of the Christian family is helpful. It makes us better and more as God would have us be. It is my hope that this dialogue with a United Methodist Bishop will be a launching pad for more dialogue.

A SHORT PAUSE

It is necessary to state the truth concerning my experience in the United Methodist Church. In my thirty-plus years as a member,

17. Merriam-Webster, "Ghosting."

volunteer, and later, pastor in the United Methodist Church, I have met many amazing and faithful Christians who live their faith everyday. I have only met a few laity in the churches I have served that would agree with Sprague on issues like the resurrection of Jesus. I would be able to fit them on both hands. At the same time, within leadership of the church and academia within the church, I could easily get to both hands and feet of people who deny the bodily resurrection of Jesus.

This will be the new debate within the United Methodist Church. I do not believe most laity or clergy understand the debate to come since the debate on marriage has dominated the discussion. There is an expression, "The enemy of my enemy is my friend." Sadly, this is how the debate on marriage was often framed. Now that the debate on marriage has been settled within the United Methodist Church, however, it is only a matter of time before the debate on the resurrection will arise.

QUESTIONS FOR REVIEW, REFLECTION, AND DISCUSSION

1. When and where did Joseph Sprague serve as a Bishop in the United Methodist Church?
2. How does Sprague describe progressive theology?
3. What does Sprague mean by neoliteralism?
4. How does Sprague re-interpret the atonement?
5. What are some predictable outcomes of Sprague's thesis?

Struggles with Science

*O Lord, our Sovereign, how majestic is
your name in all the earth!*

PSALM 8:1

REV. DR. MARTIN LUTHER King Jr. provides wisdom when speaking about the roles and benefits of both science and religion. King writes in his book *Strength to Love*, which includes a sermon titled, "A Tough Mind and a Tender Heart,"

> Science investigates; religion interprets. Science gives man knowledge and power; religion gives man wisdom which is control. Science deals mainly with facts; religion deals mainly with values. The two are not rivals. They are complimentary. Science keeps religion from sinking into the valley of crippling irrationalism and paralyzing obscurantism. Religion prevents science from falling into the marsh of obsolete materialism and moral nihilism.[1]

As a Christian pastor, I see God in creation. Creation itself, life itself, is a revelation of a creative, life giving and loving God. Science is then a gift and a tool to examine creation and in so doing grow in our knowledge and wonder of God.

Why then does progressive theology struggle with science? Have you noticed how many scientific issues and scientific claims

---

1. King, *Strength to Love*, 3–4.

are now debated in the realm of public opinion and the court system, rather than being scrutinized on the means of scientific merit? A few examples, though not an exhaustive list, would include abortion, post-abortion syndrome, global warming (now called climate change) and women's sports. All these issues are politicized and open dialogue seeking greater understanding in many cases is vilified.

For the purpose of this book I am going to focus on climate change. For some, discussing climate change and the need to save the planet and life upon it, is a closed discussion.

However, if we are seeking knowledge in a scientific arena, questions are necessary. Climate change has always occurred on planet earth and will always be occurring. One of my favorite places to visit, refresh, and retreat is the Hocking Hills near Logan, Ohio. The hills are beautiful. Life abounds. There are creeks and caves, including Old Man's Cave, and huge boulders that randomly dot the landscape. These hills, caves, and boulders are all remnants of the last Ice Age.

It is believed that the continents were once connected by large land bridges, thus leading to the migration of peoples and the populating of the continents. Antarctica was once a tropical forest. The truth of climate change is undeniable. The effect of human activity on climate change is a valid question.

If after rigorous study and debate, it is determined that human activity is moving the planet and those living on the planet to extinction, and if the decision is made to change the world economy as a result of global warming and the effects of global change, then it is appropriate to ask what these implications might entail. Obviously, there would be untold wealth both lost and gained. Stating this truth, is it not valid to follow the money so that human nature found in greed and power does not find unexpected and fertile ground to grow?

Is it not a valid question to ask how a shift in the world economy may affect underdeveloped regions of the world? Will a shift lead to new opportunities and prosperity or will it relegate these regions to another season of exploitation, despair, and poverty?

Do You Still Believe in Miracles?

I am not a scientist, nor am I a politician. I am a Christian pastor; therefore, my role is not to debate the merit of scientific study on climate change, abortion, post-abortion syndrome, and women's sports. My role is to offer insights and draw upon the wisdom of those like Rev. Dr. Martin King Jr. thus encouraging creativity, questioning, study, and dialogue, since I believe these are gifts from God and can bring us closer to God and more in harmony with each other.

The definition of the scientific method reads "principles and procedures for the systematic pursuit of knowledge involving the recognition and formulation of a problem, the collection of data through observation and experiment, and the formulation and testing of hypotheses."[2]

A problem occurs in progressive theology, beginning with Rudolf Bultmann (1884–1976). Sprague wrote concerning his theological education at MTSO that it was "steeped in the demythologizing methodology of Rudolf Bultmann."[3] Rooted in a desire to make the teaching of the New Testament relevant for the modern mind, it was believed that a God acting through miracles could no longer be useful. Further, in the aftermath of the atrocities of World War II, it was believed that a benevolent and loving God who acts in the world could never allow such brutality. It was believed that the scientific mind would eventually answer all the mysteries of the universe and root out simplistic superstitions.

Sprague writes,

> While God was never declared dead at MTSO or from any pulpit behind which I stood, surely the god of classical theism—an essentially male, impregnating Being out there somewhere, who either started it all and backed off or who controls it by indistinguishable behavior altered occasionally, even miraculously, by certain prayers and supernatural interventions—was dead because that god never really existed except in the minds of the fanciful or superstitious.[4]

2. Merriam-Webster, "Scientific Method."
3. Sprague, *Affirmation of a Dissenter*, 94.
4. Sprague, *Affirmation of a Dissenter*, 17–18.

My point is not to debate Sprague on issues that we would clearly disagree on. My point is to highlight the incongruence of Bultmann, Sprague, and thinkers like them with scientific methodology. Scientific methodology does not begin with a conclusion and then connect the dots to the desired conclusion. Beginning with the premise that God does not act. God does not act in miraculous ways. The Red Sea is simply a story. The bodily resurrection of Jesus from the dead is a myth. The witness of the faithful is nothing less than delusion, superstition, and zealotry denies the openness, questions, and criticism of the scientific method.

Science is questioning the claim that modern thinkers must deny miracles to be smart and intellectual. Science being consistent with its own methodology is actually, under further examination and criticism, beginning to understand that the dismissal of ideas and wisdom not yet understood is not "not very smart and intellectual."

In the article "How Intellectuals Found God," Peter Savodnik explores this fascinating phenomena occurring among several of today's "intellectuals." Savodnik writes,

> For more than a century, the people at the apex of the so-called thinking classes had insisted that, post-Enlightenment, it was impossible to believe in God. Not all of them put it as bluntly as Friedrich Nietzsche did in his 1882 work *The Gay Science*, in which he declared that "God is dead." Nor did they attempt to dismantle the whole religious project the way philosopher Bertrand Russell did in his 1927 essay, "Why I Am Not a Christian," arguing that religion is based "mainly on fear."[5]

At another time in the article, Savodnik writes,

> But something profound is happening. Instead of smirking at religion, some of our most important philosophers, novelists, and public intellectuals are now reassessing their contempt for it. They are wondering if they might have missed something. Religion, the historian Niall

---

5. Savodnik, "How Intellectuals Found God."

Do You Still Believe in Miracles?

Ferguson told me, "provides ethical immunity for the false religions of Lenin and Hitler."[6]

This shift among many intellectuals is happening, in part, due to the world of science, which is demonstrating with an ever-quickening pace that the more we humans think we know, the more worlds of knowledge we realize we have never even begun to know. And the more we might see chaos in creation, the more that we begin to understand the possibility of order in the chaos.[7]

The neurosurgeon Eben Alexander discusses his own near-death experience in his book *Proof of Heaven: A Neurosurgeon's Journey into the Afterlife*.

> Science-the science of which I have devoted so much of my life-doesn't contradict what I learned up there. But far, far too many people believe it does, certain members of the scientific community, who are pledged to the materialistic worldview, have insisted again and again that science and spirituality cannot exist. They are mistaken.[8]

Later, Eben writes concerning his personal experience and the inconsistency with science within the prevailing notion to simply dismiss near-death experiences within science's own methodology of inquiry.

> Medically speaking, that I have recovered completely was a flat-out impossibility, a medical miracle. But the real story lay where I had been, and I had a duty not just as a scientist and a profound respecter of the scientific method, but also as a healer to tell that story. A story—a true story—can heal as much as medicine can.[9]

These scientific areas of study, to name a few, point to the reality of mystery beyond human understanding. Some would say this is a freeing, life-giving conclusion for human seekers, since it understands that the individual self, we humans, are not the center

---

6. Savodnik, "How Intellectuals Found God."
7. Begley, "Science Finds God."
8. Alexander, *Proof of Heaven*, 72–73.
9. Alexander, *Proof of Heaven*, 144.

of the universe who must fix all the problems of the world. Rather, we are not alone. Mystery is part of existence. Creative, life-giving love lives!

QUESTIONS FOR REVIEW, REFLECTION, AND DISCUSSION

1. How does Rev. Dr. Martin Luther King Jr. describe the benefit of both science and religion?
2. What is the root of the problem within progressive theology with science and the scientific method?
3. What are two areas of scientific inquiry that are moving the debate concerning the dismissal of spirituality and mystery?

Grace and Truth

Revisiting Membership Trends

*God saw everything that he had made,
and indeed, it was very good.*

GENESIS 1:31A

THIS CHAPTER WILL RE-EXAMINE membership trends as first explored in chapter three, "Inclusiveness and Universality." First is an examination of membership trends seen in the six denominations that at one time belonged to the Religious Coalition for Reproductive Choice and six denominations that do not promote or condone abortion. Second, a re-examination of membership trends in denominations that allow the ordination of women as clergy and denominations that do not allow the ordination of women as clergy.

The denominations that at one point joined the Religious Coalition for Reproductive Choice are American Baptist USA, Christian Church (Disciples of Christ), Episcopalian Church in the United States, Presbyterian Church USA, United Church of Christ, and the United Methodist Church. The United Methodist Church will not be included within this analysis of membership trends for two reasons. First, on May 19, 2016, at the General Conference of the United Methodist Church, the United Methodist Church voted to withdraw from the Religious Coalition for

Reproductive Choice.[1] Second, the United Methodist Church has experienced a schism, and current membership numbers may not accurately reflect the views of members and churches who may be in the process of disaffiliation.

These are the membership trends for the American Baptist Church USA, Christian Church (Disciples of Christ), Episcopalian Church in the United States, Presbyterian Church USA, and the United Church of Christ.

American Baptist Church USA	1,400,000 (2004)	1,211,744[2] (2023)
Christian Church (Disciples of Christ)	786,334 (2002)	350,618[3] (2020)
Episcopalian Church in the United States	2,320,221 (2002)	1,547,779[4] (2023)
Presbyterian Church USA	2,525,330 (2000)	1,245,354[5] (2020)
United Church of Christ	1,330.985 (2002)	773,539[6] (2020)

Following the same line of thinking stated earlier in this book, that God will bless and grow Christian communities that are attached to the living vine of Christ and that God will allow Christian communities to wither and even die when the community has chosen to detach itself from the Bible, Christian tradition, and the Christian witness throughout the ages, it is apparent that all six denominations that joined the Religious Coalition for Reproductive Choice have experienced and continue to experience dramatic loss in membership since choosing that path.

In the chapter "Abortion and Truth" and using data found within that chapter, there were a total of 10,750,362 combined members in the American Baptist Church USA, Christian Church (Disciples of Christ), Episcopalian Church in the United States, Presbyterian Church USA, and United Church of Christ in 1975.

1. Stallsworth, "United Methodist Church Leaves."
2. https://baptistworld.org/.
3. www.disciples.org.
4. Episcopal Church, "2023 Parochial Report."
5. pcusa.org.
6. www.ucc.org.

At the time I first completed this apologetic in 2008 the combined membership of these denominations was 8,362,870 members. Current data reveals 5,379,297 combined membership.

To restate the working principle of this examination of membership trends, it is imperative to state truth with grace. A decline in membership does not reflect a lack of faith within individual members. God will continue to meet faithfulness with faithfulness and bless the lives of individuals within these faith communities. What I am suggesting is that examining membership trends may give us a glimpse into God's will. God's will is to bring about salvation and our role as followers of Jesus is to do our part in ushering in the kingdom of God.

I will continue to examine membership trends by examining the same six denominations found in the chapter "Abortion and Truth" that have chosen to promote the view that God is active in life and life begins at conception. These denominations include the African Methodist Episcopal Zion Church, Assemblies of God, Church of the Nazarene, Presbyterian Church in America, Roman Catholic Church and Southern Baptist Convention.

African Methodist Episcopal Zion Church	1,430,795 (2002)	1,400,000+[7] (2024)
Assemblies of God	2,687,266 (2002)	3,000,000[8] (2024)
Church of the Nazarene	639,330 (2002)	650,000[9] (2020)
Presbyterian Church in America	310,750 (2002)	383,338[10] (2020)
Roman Catholic Church	67,515,016 (2007)	73,200,000[11] (2021)
Southern Baptist Church	16,247,736 (2002)	12,982,090[12] (2022)

7. ame-church.com.
8. ag.org.
9. nazarene.org.
10. PCA.org.
11. Center for Applied Research in the Apostolate 1970–2021.
12. sbc.net.

Examining these membership trends, we find that five of six of these denominations experienced modest growth in membership or maintained current membership in the United States. The African Methodist Episcopal Zion Church, Assemblies of God, Church of the Nazarene, Presbyterian Church in America and the Roman Catholic Church all continued to maintain or grow in membership. The combined membership of these five denominations in the early 1970s was 51,237,755. When this apologetic was first completed in 2008, the combined membership of these five denominations was 72,583,157. The most recent combined membership of these five denominations is 78,633,338 in the United States.

It is interesting to note that both the African Methodist Episcopal Zion Church and the Assemblies of God reveal amazing growth in their communities when speaking of membership from a world perspective. The African Methodist Episcopal Zion Church records more than 2,785,000 members worldwide[13] and the Assemblies of God number 86,143,293 members worldwide.[14] God continues to be active and blesses communities of faith with membership growth.

The Southern Baptist Convention membership trends require further examination beyond the purpose of this book. In 1975, the total membership within the Southern Baptist Convention was 12,067,284, this grew to 16,247,736 in 2002, and has fallen to 12,982,090 members in 2022.

Returning to an examination of membership trends among denominations that ordain women as clergy and denominations that do not ordain women as clergy. In the chapter "Inclusiveness and Universality," the membership trends of nine denominations that ordain women as clergy, the African Methodist Episcopal Zion Church, American Baptist Church USA, Assemblies of God, Christian Church (Disciples of Christ), Church of the Nazarene, Episcopalian Church in the United States, Presbyterian Church

---

13. ame-church.com
14. ag.org

USA, the United Church of Christ, and the United Methodist Church.

Current membership trends within these denominations reinforces findings found in the chapter "Inclusivity and Universality," that the ordination of women as clergy is not a consistent indicator of church membership growth or loss. Current membership data continues the trend that the American Baptist Church USA, Christian Church (Disciples of Christ), the United Church of Christ, the Episcopalian Church in the United States, and the Presbyterian Church USA have all declined in membership growth. The African Methodist Episcopal Zion Church, Assemblies of God, Church of the Nazarene have all maintained or grown in membership.

The United Methodist Church will be an interesting trend to follow in the future since the United Methodist Church and the newly break-away denomination the Global Methodist Church both affirm the ordination of women.

QUESTIONS FOR REVIEW, REFLECTION, AND DISCUSSION

1. Between 1975 and the most current data, which of the twelve denominations examined grew in membership and which denominations decreased in membership?
2. What are common factors in these trends?
3. Was the ordination of women a consistent indicator in membership trends? Explain.

Jesus Is Good News

The beginning of the good news of Jesus Christ.
MARK 1:1

FOR THE CHRISTIAN, JESUS is the truth (John 14:6) and all persons are invited to be in relationship with the One who is truth. In this way, truth is an experienced relationship. It is a way of life that gives life to life itself. Jesus is revealed truth, a gift to all, and accessible to all. Jesus is the Savior of the World (John 4:42). For the Christian this is good news that deserves to be shared.

The question, "What is truth?" is an eternal question. While interrogating Jesus shortly before the crucifixion, Pontius Pilate asks Jesus, "What is truth? (John 18:38). Definitions of the word truth include: 1) the state of being true; 2) that which is true, actual facts; 3) a fact or belief that is accepted as true.[1]

The quest for truth and the claim of some to have ownership of truth has a long history. One form of thought is Gnosticism which is found as early as 1 AD. "Gnostic Christians, claimed to have 'secret knowledge' about the nature of the universe, the nature of Christ, and what his appearance on earth meant to believers."[2]

The concept of secret knowledge that is only known by an enlightened few and the gift of revealed truth accessible and given to all has a profound impact on how a person understands God,

---

1. *Pocket Oxford American Dictionary*, 894.
2. Denova, "Gnosticism."

the nature of self, the concept of community, and ultimately the value of life. Does all life have value or only some lives? Do some lives have more value due to one's level of enlightenment?

Historically gnosticism has challenged traditional Christian orthodox faith in various ways. One example was addressed by Irenaeus (130–202 AD) and the struggle with early Gnosticism which sought to demote the creator God to a second and inferior status. Marianne Meye Thompson writes, "Irenaeus combats the Gnostics who wished to sever the God who created from the God who saves."[3]

Today's gnosticism has moved from the concept of secret knowledge or secret truth known only to the few enlightened, to the idea that there is simply no truth. There is no objective truth. It is to the concept of no truth that I speak truth.

Some would claim that there is no Jesus of Nazareth. It is all a story. A delusion. A myth that has no historical foundation. This argument lacks intellectual integrity. Would anyone question if Cleopatra lived? Would anyone question if Napoleon lived? Cleopatra lived from 69 BC to 30 BC. Napoleon was born August 15, 1769, and died May 5, 1821. These are objective facts of history. What their lives meant is open to discussion and debate. However, the argument that they never lived is undeniable.

In a similar way, an argument against the life of a historical Jesus lacks intellectual integrity. He lived at a certain time in history. His life is a fact of history. Further, the fact that some followed and believed in Jesus is also a fact of history. What it means, again, is open to discussion and debate. However, the fact that Jesus lived and people still talk about him is a statement of truth.

To those who claim there is no truth is the undeniable reality of objective truth. History is an example of truth as actual facts.

Faith is a belief that is accepted as true. And for the Christian who is in relationship with a risen Savior it becomes a living truth. Truth has a name.

---

3. Thompson, "Gospel of John," 154–66.

MY TRUTH

It is not uncommon to hear some say, "My truth." However, what does that mean and what does that not mean? First, the comment "my truth" does not negate the reality of objective truth as discussed above. There is objective truth. The fact that Cleopatra, Napoleon, and Jesus lived reflects objective truth.

At the same time, the statement "my truth" can be very empowering and healing for individuals and communities. It is a statement that validates a lived experience. One of the definitions stated earlier read, "a statement or belief that is accepted as true."

In my own life learning to claim "my truth" was a time of healing. In my early thirties I was an ordained elder in the church and I was serving a three point charge in Wisconsin. I had a counselor/spiritual director which I found to be very helpful. I remember one day we were talking, and I used the phrase "Anger is a negative emotion." My counselor/spiritual director asked me what I meant by negative emotion and this led to a whole new level of understanding and healing.

As we worked on this concept for the next few months I was able to understand that my truth that anger is a negative emotion was stinky thinking that needed to be discarded so that I could develop a healthier understanding of anger. As a survivor of pre-cognitive PTSD, I had experienced very negative uses of anger in my early developmental years. As I grew older I determined that I did not have the luxury to express my anger for fear that I might demonstrate anger in similar ways that I had experienced.

As it worked out, this meant I was not always easy to get along with and at times I might act in passive aggressive ways. The first thing I needed to do was understand the truth that all people get angry. It is a neutral emotion, like all emotions. Jesus became angry (Matt 21:12–17, Mark 11:15–19, Luke 19:45–48 and John 2:13–17).

As we continued to work, John 1:17—"Grace and truth came through Jesus Christ"—became a way of making some peace with the past and also a new way to navigate the future. I learned that the sooner I get to truth (my truth), the sooner I could get to grace to others and myself.

It can be healing and a gift to hear another person's "my truth." At the same time, it is important to remember that no one has ownership of truth. God is free and can act in ways beyond human comprehension.

QUESTIONS FOR REVIEW, REFLECTION AND DISCUSSION

1. What is a definition of "Gnosticism?"
2. What is a modern form of Gnosticism?
3. How is history an example of truth understood as "actual facts"?
4. How does the statement "my truth" differ from objective truth? How might claiming "my truth" be healing for individuals and communities?

Glimpses of God

And remember I am with you to the end of the age.
MATTHEW 28:20

MANY TIMES ONE HEARS critics of Christianity critique the Christian faith based on history. These can be valid critiques as Christian mistakes have occurred within the church and in the name of Jesus. The Spanish Inquisition and the Salem Witch Trials come to mind. These atrocities are important reminders that we are flawed and therefore in need of God's grace and guidance. Oftentimes, we can learn more from our mistakes than from the times we get things right.

In this regard, it is also valid within the realms of intellectual integrity to discuss times within history when the Christian community and the church might have got it right. Meaning that inspired by Jesus, communities and societies have sought to reflect the kingdom of God within their culture and society. I am going to spend some time reflecting upon five occasions where the Christian faithful have worked to reflect the kingdom of God as taught by Jesus within their society.

First, let us reflect upon the frontier of North America in the 1700s. An important decision needed to be made by the Christian community. In many cases, individual groups and families would settle on the frontier before clergy and a more structured form of church arrived. The decision made by many early settlers was to

Do You Still Believe in Miracles?

bring their Bible and to read their Bible. This would have been a liberal, even scandalous idea for people to read their Bible on their own and without clergy present. As communities developed, another decision would need to be made. Who would be taught to read? Often the driving force for literacy on the American frontier was a desire for people to be able to read their Bible. However, would boys and girls be taught to read? Again, a liberal, even scandalous decision was made when it was decided by many that both little boys and little girls (regardless of their income status) would be taught to read.[1]

I believe this is a time the Christian community got it right and this gift from the Christian faith is now a given within many communities throughout the world. Yes, all little boys and all little girls having the opportunity to read is a good thing.

For most of human history the institution of slavery was understood as a symbol of one's power and wealth. Slavery can be seen all around the world and throughout human history. Even today slavery can be found. However, in most situations slavery is now seen as a moral evil. Why did it change?

It is impossible to examine the change within most societies that now understand slavery as a moral evil without acknowledging the contributions of the Christian faithful on the issue of slavery. William Wilberforce (August 24, 1759—July 29, 1833) was born in England at a time when the slave trade was very active and profitable. Wilberforce converted to evangelical Christianity in 1784–85 and his faith would become a driving force behind him becoming an abolitionist.[2] Wilberforce wrote in his diary on October 28, 1787, God had sent him two great objects: the suppression of the slave trade and the work for moral reform.[3]

In his book *Real Christianity*, Wilberforce wrote, "All of us have the obligation to do whatever we are able to do to promote the welfare of our fellowman."[4] Later he wrote, "The goal is to use

1. See Phares, *Bible in Pocket*.
2. Britannica, "William Wilberforce."
3. Wilberforce, *Real Christianity*, 11.
4. Wilberforce, *Real Christianity*, 17.

those abilities we possess for the right purposes. We are to employ them for the advancement of God's plans and purposes."[5]

Wilberforce would dedicate much of his life to the struggle to end the slave trade and abolish slavery in Britain and all the British overseas possessions. On February 23, 1807, under Wilberforce's leadership a bill to abolish the slave trade in the British West Indies was carried in the Commons. It would become law on March 25, 1807.[6] Much later in Wilberforce's life and after much struggle, slavery would end in the British Empire. "On July 26, 1833 the Slavery Abolition Act was passed by the Commons (it became law the following month). Three days later Wilberforce died."[7]

There was a time in American history where the thought of women voting would have been considered offensive and absurd. The first amendment introduced in Congress to give women the right to vote happened in 1878; however, it was not ratified until August 18, 1920. The 19th Amendment to the U.S. Constitution:—Women's Right to Vote (1920)—enshrined the right for women to vote.[8] This is a time where the Christian community assisted in moving society in a way to more reflect the kingdom of God and the innate dignity in all persons.

In 1836, Wesleyan College in Macon, GA, became the first women's college in the world. A year later Oberlin College, in Oberlin, OH, became the first college to open its doors to men and women.[9]

One can only wonder what impact the decision to teach little girls to read in the early 1700s might have had on the eventual recognition of a woman's right to vote. It is reasonable to think that literacy among women had a profound effect on women eventually earning the right to vote in the United States.

Two women, Helen Keller (June 27, 1880—June 1, 1968) and Annie Sullivan (April 14, 1866—October 20, 1936), forever

5. Wilberforce, *Real Christianity*, 92.
6 "William Wilberforce."
7. "William Wilberforce."
8. "19th Amendment."
9. National University, "Women in Higher Education."

changed the way many throughout the world see people with disabilities and special needs. Before these two women of faith who possessed profound courage and resilience, people with disabilities and special needs were often seen as a liability or a drain upon limited resources instead of a person with innate dignity and gifts to give to the greater good. Persons who reflect the divine spark found in all.

Helen was blind and deaf due to a childhood illness. As a young woman, before her days at Radcliffe College, Helen wrote,

> Such knowledge floods the soul unseen with a soundless tidal wave of deepening thought. "Knowledge is power." Rather, knowledge is happiness, because to have knowledge—broad, deep knowledge—is to know true ends from false, and lofty things from low. To know the thoughts and deeds that have marked man's progress is to feel the great heart-throbs of humanity through the centuries; and if one does not feel in these pulsations a heavenward striving, one must indeed be deaf to the harmonies of life.[10]

Rev. Dr. Martin Luther King Jr. (January 15, 1929—April 4, 1968), a Baptist preacher, changed race relations in the United States. His persistent call for civil rights among all citizens through peaceful protest left an indelible impression on the country and the strive to more faithfully reflect the kingdom of God among all races and the innate dignity known in all people.

King spoke these words in a sermon he preached titled, "A Tough Mind and a Tender Heart,"

> Violence brings only temporary victories; violence, by creating many more social problems than it solves, never brings permanent peace. I am convinced that if we succumb to the temptation to use violence in our struggle for freedom, unborn generations will be the recipients of a long and desolate night of bitterness, and our chief legacy to them will be a never-ending reign of chaos. A voice, echoing through the corridors of time, says to

---

10. Keller. *Story of My Life*, 90.

every intemperate Peter, "Put up thy sword." History is cluttered with the wreckage of nations that failed to follow Christ's command.[11]

Each of these examples are times within human history when the Christian community sought to reflect an understanding of the kingdom of God into their society. In each case, there would be struggle and resistance. However, grounded by faith, change occurred. I am someone who believes each of these examples, though liberal and often offensive to some, were faithful struggles of their day and a gift for future generations and to the world.

MIRACLES

The definition of miracle reads "an extraordinary and welcome event believed to be the work of God."[12] In this regard the purpose of a miracle is to tell us something about God, to reveal something about the nature of God. It may be that God gives life or there is healing in God or there is a peace that passes understanding in Christ or in Christ there is freedom and new life. This is not an exhaustive list. Miracles reveal God is with us and God's mystery is beyond our understanding.

A problem occurs with an understanding of miracles commonly along three lines of thinking. First, miracles can be understood in a transactional way of relating to God. In this way, the individual may make a bargain with God. "I will do this and you (God) will do . . ." Fill in the blank. Another transactional way of relating to God would be, "God if you act in the way I want (for example heal a person I love) then I will do . . ." Fill in the blank.

Second is an understanding of miracles that can resemble a genie in a bottle way of relating to God. If I perform a certain gesture, pray a certain prayer, donate a certain amount of money to the church, then I will get the miracle of my dreams. A problem with this way of relating to God is it seems to assume that the

---

11. King. *Strength to Love*, 7.
12. *Pocket Oxford American Dictionary*, 522.

person is in control of God when in reality God is free and therefore able to act in ways that may be mysterious and even beyond our understanding.

Third is the lament that others may have gotten their miracle, "Then why didn't I?" This is an honest human reaction to pain and loss and can be an initial step of healing. However, if a person remains stuck in this way of relating to God, angry, hurt, and grieving, they will remain angry, hurt and grieving until they realize the miracle being experienced is God faithfully being with us in our anger, pain and grief. God's promise is to be with us and perhaps in the midst of the anger, pain, and grief we come to a new realization "that love never ends" (1 Cor 13:8) or "We are surrounded by a great cloud of witnesses" (Heb 12:1) or "I have prepared a place for you" (John 14:2).

Some say that miracles do not happen. That God does not exist therefore God does not act. To this train of thought I simply offer stories from my own life experience and God being active in my life. I am going to recount three events; though I could share others. I am going to focus on God working in life, God working in death and God working in mystery.

I experienced the miracle of life at the age of twenty-five. My first child was born at thirty-four and a half weeks at three pounds and seven ounces. My wife was on bed rest at a hospital for a month with preeclampsia. This was in the year 1990. When my son was born there was two ounces of amniotic fluid. I watched a nurse wipe it up with a paper towel. Sometimes it is good to be young and dumb. It was not until years later that it dawned on me that he was literally kept alive by two ounces of amniotic fluid.

At six foot and four inches, I am a rather big guy, and for the first few months I literally had to hold him in my hands. He had very little muscle tone and he was too floppy to hold in my arms. I held him in my hands. His head was the size of an egg and fit into the palm of my right hand and his bottom was in my left hand. That is how I held him and rocked him. In these moments I came to understand that God is active in life and I was holding a miracle.

For nearly twenty years of my ministry, I have been a hospital chaplain. My primary appointment has been the emergency department, two Intensive Care units, and eventually covering whatever is needed within all parts of the hospital. In this way, I have served primarily as a crisis chaplain. We respond to every death, code blue, trauma (we are a trauma hospital), STEMI (heart attack), hemorrhagic stroke, respiratory stat, early fetal loss, and every baby death. We are also often called to be a supportive presence during a palliative extubation and movement to comfort care, and a patient and family's hospice journey. This means over the years I have been called to attend to tens of thousands of crisis situations. Around three thousand times, these situations would mean providing ministry to loved ones at the time of death. This includes well over five hundred sudden deaths in the emergency department. Being around death and the mystery of death is simply a part of the job of a crisis chaplain. It also means I have been asked—in many, many situations—to be with a person on the worst day of their life. I will share one of those situations.

I was working a night shift at the hospital and responded to a trauma alert. When I arrived at the trauma bay, I was informed that we were expecting a patient who was the victim of a gunshot. The trauma team assembled and soon medics wheeled the patient into the bay. We learned the patient was a young woman who had been shot in the back of the head. The patient was extremely critical.

When turning the patient there was a sound that I will never forget. A game controller fell out of her hand and landed on the floor. She must have been playing a video game when she was shot in the back of the head. The medical team did all that they could but there was nothing they could do to save her life. They bandaged her head and she was moved to an intensive care unit. Her brain was continuing to swell and she was going to die.

The police left the hospital to return to the scene to try and locate any next-of-kin. Later in the night, I was called by the nurse informing me that the mother of the patient had arrived and she was requesting a chaplain for prayer. I went to be with the mother and her daughter knowing I was called to be with her on the worst day of her life. When I arrived, I introduced myself. She was gazing lovingly at her daughter and she asked me to pray. We prayed over her daughter and then sat together in the room. She told a few stories of her daughter, however, most of the time we sat in silence. Later, that night the patient died.

As I have reflected upon this experience all I can say is God was with us. God was with that mother in the midst of unimaginable pain and she experienced some sense of comfort even on the worst day of her life.

In my ministry for over thirty years as a pastor and later a chaplain, I have experienced the mystery of God on many occasions. I am going to share one story from the bedside that I experienced as a hospital chaplain.

It was a Monday morning and I was called by the nurse. She explained to me that there was a planned extubation and move to comfort care for a patient and the patient had a son who was in the room alone. I stopped before entering the room and learned several days earlier that the patient had experienced a devastating, non-survivable stroke. The doctors determined she was too unstable to do brain death testing and wanted to give family the opportunity to be at the bedside when the patient died.

I met her son. (I will call him Mike.) Mike seemed anxious and paced as preparations were being made by the medical team. We spoke and I learned the patient had three children. Mike explained that his older sister had been to the hospital to be with the patient the previous night and they had decided to say their last good-bye at that time. During the night, however, he felt a need to return. This explained why he was in the room alone. Mike also told me he had a younger sister who died at the age of seven and that his father had died a few years ago.

The patient was extubated. Mike stood holding his mother's left hand. The nurse and I stood at the foot of the bed silently. Then something unexplainable occurred. The patient who had not moved since the devastating stroke slowly raised her right hand and moved it in a motion like giving someone a hug. She lowered her arm and then began to raise her right arm again. This time her arm was lower, more at the waist area. She then lowered her arm and died.

The room was silent and felt holy. A person cannot experience something like that and be the same. Something happened and the three of us in the room witnessed it. I believe we witnessed God's mystery and Mike believed his mother was giving a hug to both his father and younger sister.

QUESTIONS FOR REVIEW, REFLECTION, AND DISCUSSION

1. The author suggests culture and society can reflect the kingdom of God. Do you agree or disagree with this premise? Explain.

2. Ruiz examines five occasions where the Christian faithful have worked to reflect the kingdom of God as taught by Jesus within society. What are your thoughts on his perspective? Explain.

3. Have you ever experienced a miracle? How might your answer to this question influence your understanding of God?

Life is Better with Jesus

I am the way, the truth, and the life.

JOHN 14:6

THROUGHOUT THIS BOOK I have proclaimed that God is alive! God is active in the world, in the lives of people, in society, and throughout history. Further, I have argued that for the Christian God is best understood through the life, death and resurrection of Jesus and God's continuing activity and faithfulness that are revealed when we seek to have the eyes to see God's activity.

With this as a foundation of truth, the Christian community proclaiming the life, death, and resurrection of Jesus answers the three most prominent questions and issues experienced by young people in our society. I believe these issues are meaning in life, a clear understanding of truth, and a desire for community.

The well known thinker Walter Brueggemann writes in his book *Hope for the World* concerning the need for Jesus. Brueggemann writes for "human community not defined by commodity." Brueggemann suggests that "despair is the defining mark of the context for the church in the twenty-first century" and the Christian community, as a "community of hope," must engage this reality.[1]

It seems that meaning in life seems hard to find for many of our young people. Many within our society have lived their whole lives with internet access, email accounts, and smartphones. In

---

1. Brueggemann, *Hope for the World*, 155.

some ways, these mediating technologies have unleashed a wave of creativity and a connection and appreciation for various people and cultures around the world that were simply unavailable and unimaginable before these technologies came into existence. At the same time, having access to news around the world twenty-four/seven can also make the world seem more chaotic and scary. Where is their meaning? For without meaning, existence, life itself, can become a form of anxiety, depressing and meaningless. Could this be a reason for the increase in anxiety issues, suicides, and declining birth rates in many areas of the world?

A recent article titled "Feeling anxious? Understanding the Rise in Anxiety Disorders Among Young Adults" reports,

> Anxiety affects young adults at a much higher rate than older generations. The Population Reference Bureau found that in 2022, over 40% of adults ages 18–29 reported symptoms of anxiety more days than not, compared to 16% of adults over 60.[2]

The Bulletin on Health reports that between 2000 and 2020, the U.S. suicide rate exhibited an upward trend. Between 2000 and 2020, the suicide rate rose from ten per 100,000 to just over fourteen—a 40 percent increase in only twenty years.[3] Another article published by the University of Colorado–Boulder reported that nearly 50,000 people in the U.S. took their own lives in 2022, up 3 percent from the previous year.[4]

A recent report from the CDC, National Center for Health Statistics reported,

> The general fertility rate in the United States decreased by 3% from 2022, reaching a historic low. This marks the second consecutive year of decline, following a brief 1% increase from 2020 to 2021. From 2014 to 2020, the rate consistently decreased by 2% annually.[5]

2. Hunt, "Feeling Anxious?"
3. Bulletin on Health, "Rise in Suicide Rates."
4. Marshall, "Suicide Rates in the US."
5. CDC National Center for Health Statistics, "U.S. Fertility Rates Drop to Another Historic Low"

Do You Still Believe in Miracles?

Jesus said, "I am the way" (John 14:6a). For the Christian, Jesus as the way provides meaning in life. "The true light, which enlightens everyone, was coming into the world" (John 1:9). This means, from a Christian perspective, every life has meaning in the eyes of God. Is it any wonder that Rick Warren's book *The Purpose Driven Life*[6] would become a best-seller and have millions of copies purchased throughout the world.

Addressing the difficulty of truth, the Christian believer points to Jesus himself. Jesus said, "I am the way and the truth" (John 14:a). In the chapter "Jesus is Good News," I discussed at length the importance of truth and a Christian understanding of truth.

Many young people struggle with a desire for community. While the internet, emails, and smartphones have provided access to ideas, cultures, and news previously unimaginable, it has also had the effect of making intimate human to human interactions and the development of community more difficult. In the book *The Extinction of Experience: Being Human in a Disembodied World*, Christine Rosen challenges thoughtful discourse for children and generations who have known nothing but a world with these technologies. She writes,

> This book is a modest effort to encourage us to cultivate and, in some cases, recover ways of thinking, knowing, and being in the world that we are losing or have lost through our embrace of mediating technologies.[7]

Earlier she wrote,

> In these new worlds, we are Users, not individuals. We are meant to prefer these engineered User Experiences to human reality. This book argues that we arrived here by allowing human experiences to wither or die, sometimes intentionally and sometimes unintentionally.[8] What do we gain and what do we lose when we no longer

---

6. Warren, *Purpose Driven Life*.
7. Rosen, *Extinction of Experience*, 7.
8. Rosen, *Extinction of Experience*, 4.

talk about the Human Condition, but rather the User Experience?[9]

For many young people, being ghosted (a modern day form of shaming and shunning) is seen as the worst thing imaginable. This is because for many the internet, gaming, and various forms of social media networking *is* their community. Thus ghosting leaves the individual alone and without community.

Desmond Tutu spoke into the issue of loneliness and the human need for community. Tutu wrote, "God has made us in such a way that we need each other. We are made for companionship and relationship. It is not good for us to be alone."[10]

Jesus said, "I am the way the truth and the life" (John 14:6). For the Christian a sense of community is found in a personal relationship with Jesus. God is faithful and has promised to be us always. Matthew 28:20 reads "And remember, I am with you always, to the end of the age."

Experiencing a relationship with Jesus brings a sense of personal peace since Jesus loves us, and thus one is not alone in the challenges and responsibilities that are experienced in life. This is a great antidote for the anxiety epidemic experienced by so many within our society and throughout the world.

Knowing a sense of community with God opens the believer to experience community with other Christian believers and nonbelievers because of an understanding that in God's eyes all life has meaning and value. Therefore, it is exciting to try and see those qualities in our neighbors.

Further, it is within the relationships formed in communities of fellow believers that one experiences a new type of community, a community formed by God and God's grace. The writer of the Gospel of Matthew calls it "the kingdom of God." Irwyn Ince called it "the beautiful community." Martin Luther King Jr. used the term "the beloved community." The apostle Paul calls it "the Body of Christ."

---

9. Rosen, *Extinction of Experience*, 5.
10. Tutu, *God Has a Dream*, 25.

Do You Still Believe in Miracles?

For many, including myself, some of the best and most meaningful experiences of life have been experienced within this community. I believe it is a gift from God, a gift so we may live life abundantly. "I came that they may have life, and have it abundantly" (John 10:10b).

Life is better with Jesus. I know my life has been better with Jesus. I believe your life would also be better with Jesus. Talk to him. Read one of the Gospels: Matthew, Mark, Luke or John. If you get really ambitious, read all four Gospels. The Christian life is not a spectator sport but rather is a lived reality in relationship with God known in and through Jesus.

It is an amazing adventure.

QUESTIONS FOR REVIEW, REFLECTION, AND DISCUSSION

1. What does Brueggemann describe as the defining challenge of the 21st century? What are your thoughts on his analysis?

2. Ruiz suggests meaning in life, truth and a desire for community are defining issues for young people today. What are your thoughts on his assessment?

Bibliography

"19th Amendment to the U.S. Constitution: Women's Right to Vote." National Archives, Feb 8, 2022. https://www.archives.gov/milestone-documents/19th-amendment.

"25-Year Tables." www.nemw.org/25year_tables.pdf.

"Abortion Facts, Post-Abortion Syndrome." http://www.sextruth.net/templates/System/details.asp?id=23009&PID+66342.'

Alexander, Eben. *Proof of Heaven: A Neurosurgeon's Journey into the Afterlife.* New York: Simon & Schuster, 2012.

Arinze, Francis. *Religions for Peace: A Call for Solidarity to the Religions of the World.* New York: Doubleday, 2002.

Bazelon, Emily. "Is There a Post-Abortion Syndrome?" *New York Times*, Jan 21, 2007. https://www.nytimes.com/2007/01/21/magazine/21abortion.t.html.

Begley, Sharon. "Science Finds God." *Newsweek*, July 20, 1998.

Benedict XVI. *Jesus of Nazareth*. New York: Doubleday, 2007.

Bonhoeffer, Dietrich. *Meditations on the Cross*. Edited by Manfred Weber. Louisville: Westminster John Knox, 1996.

Bristow, John Temple. *What Paul Really Said About Women: An Apostle's Liberating Views on Equality in Marriage, Leadership, and Love.* San Francisco: HarperCollins, 1998.

Britannica. "William Wilberforce." https://www.britannica.com/biography/William-Wilberforce.

Brueggemann, Walter, ed. *Hope for the World: Mission in a Global Context.* Louisville: Westminster John Knox, 2001.

Bulletin on Health. "What Accounts for the Rise in Suicide Rates in the US?" July 6, 2023. https://www.nber.org/bh/20232/what-accounts-rise-suicide-rates-us.

Bunson, Matthew, ed. *Our Sunday Visitor's Catholic Almanac 2008 Edition.* Huntington, IN: Our Sunday Visitor, 2008.

Burke, Theresa Karminski. "Abortion and Post Traumatic Stress Disorder: The Evidence Keeps Piling Up." HLI Reports.

CDC National Center for Health Statistics. "U.S. Fertility Rates Drop to Another Historic Low." Feb 15, 2024.

BIBLIOGRAPHY

Center for Applied Research in the Apostolate 1970–2021. https://cara.georgetown.edu/.

Chappell, Bill. "United Methodist Church Votes to Keep Bans." NPR, Feb 26, 2019. https://www.npr.org/2019/02/26/698188343/united-methodist-church-votes-to-keep-bans-on-same-sex-weddings-lgbtq-clergy.

Denova, Rebecca. "Gnosticism." World History Encyclopedia, Apr 9, 2021. https://www.worldhistory.org/Gnosticism/.

Edmondson, Stephen. "From a Doctor's Viewpoint." https://digitalcollections.library.gsu.edu › arwg › download.

Episcopal Church. "Episcopal Church 2023 Parochial Report Data Now Available." Nov 8, 2024. https://www.episcopalchurch.org/publicaffairs/episcopal-church-2023-parochial-report-data-now-available/.

Friedman, Ann. "The Answer Is No, 'Post-Abortion Syndrome' Doesn't Exist." Feministing, Jan 22, 2007. https://feministing.com/2007/01/22/the_answer_is_no_postabortion/.

Fuller, Cheri, and Louise Tucker Jones. *Extraordinary Kids: Nurturing and Championing Your Child With Special Needs*. Colorado Springs: Focus on Family, 1997.

"Get 'in the Know': Questions About Pregnancy, Contraception and Abortion." https://web.archive.org/web/20080208103829/www.guttmacher.org/in-the-know/incidence.html.

Girzone, Joseph. *A Portrait of Jesus*. New York: Doubleday, 1998.

Glynn, Patrick. *God: The Evidence; the Reconciliation of Faith and Reason in a Postsecular World*. Rocklin, CA: Prima Publishing, 1997.

Good News. "Message from African Delegates at 2024 General Conference." May 2, 2024. https://goodnewsmag.org/message-from-african-delegates-at-2024-general-conference/.

Grossman, Cathay Lynn. "Some Protestant Churches Feeling 'Mainline' Again." USA Today, Jan 1, 2006.

Gutierrez, Gustavo. *The God of Life*. Maryknoll, NY: Orbis, 1991.

Hahn, Heather, et al. "General Conference Gives Regionalization Green Light." UM News, Apr 25, 2024. https://www.umnews.org/en/news/regionalization-gets-general-conference-go-ahead.

Harris, Sarah. "The Number of Women Who Will Have an Abortion by Age 45." Daily Mail, Nov 5, 2001.

Hartshorne, Charles. *Omnipotence and Other Theological Mistakes*. Albany: State University of New York, 1984.

Hopper, Jeffrey. *Understanding Modern Theology I: Cultural Revolutions and New Worlds*. Philadelphia: Fortress. 1987.

———. *Understanding Modern Theology II: Reinterpreting Christian Faith for Changing Worlds*. Philadelphia: Fortress, 1989.

Hunt, Alyssa. "Feeling Anxious? Understanding the Rise of Anxiety Disorders Among Young Adults." July 17, 2024. https://news.llu.edu/health-wellness/feeling-anxious-understanding-rise-anxiety-disorders-among-young-adults.

BIBLIOGRAPHY

Ince, Irwyn I., Jr. *The Beautiful Community: Unity, Diversity, and the Church at Its Best*. Downers Grove, IL: InterVarsity, 2020.

Jenkins, Philip. *The New Faces of Christianity: Believing the Bible in the Global South*. New York: Oxford University Press, 2006.

John Paul II, Pope. *The Gospel of Life*. New York: Random House, 1995.

Johnson, Luke Timothy. *The Real Jesus: The Misguided Quest for the Historical Jesus and the Truth of the Traditional Gospels*. San Francisco: Harper Collins, 1996.

Jones, Major J. *The Color of God: The Concept of God in Afro-American Thought*. Macon, GA: Mercer University Press, 1987.

Kebler, Werner H. *Mark's Story of Jesus*. Philadelphia: Fortress, 1979.

Keller, Helen. *The Story of My Life*. Garden City, NY: Doubleday, 1954.

King, Martin Luther, Jr. *Strength to Love*. New York: Harper, 1963.

King, Ursula. *Christian Mystics: Their Lives and Legacies Throughout the Ages*. Mahwah, NJ: Hidden Springs, 2001.

Maddox, Susan. "The United Methodist Church Just Held a Historic Vote in Favor of LGBT Inclusion." CBS News, May 9, 2024. https://www.cbsnews.com/news/united-methodist-church-lgbt-regionalization-vote-whats-next/.

Major, Brenda. "Pro-Choice Researchers Acknowledge Existence of Postabortion Syndrome." After Abortion, Aug 24, 2000. https://afterabortion.org/pro-choice-researchers-acknowledge-existence-of-postabortion-syndrome/.

Marshall, Lisa. "Suicide Rates in the US Are on the Rise: New Study Offers Surprising Reasons Why." CU Boulder Today, Feb 15, 2024. https://www.colorado.edu/today/2024/02/15/suicide-rates-us-are-rise-new-study-offers-surprising-reasons-why#:~:text=But%20a%20new%20CU%20Boulder,during%20tough%20economic%20times%2C%20othe.

McFague, Sallie. *Models of God: Theology for an Ecological, Nuclear Age*. Philadelphia: Fortress, 1988.

McPolin, James. *John*. New Testament Message 6. Wilmington, DE: Michael Glazier, 1979.

Mead, Frank S., et al. *Handbook of Denominations in the United States*. 6th ed. Nashville: Abingdon, 1975.

———. *Handbook of Denominations in the United States*. 10th ed. Nashville: Abingdon, 1995.

———. *Handbook of Denominations in the United States*. 12th ed. Nashville: Abingdon, 2005.

Merriam-Webster. "Ghosting." https://www.merriam-webster.com/dictionary/ghosting.

———. "Scientific Method." https://www.merriam-webster.com/dictionary/scientific%20method.

National Right to Life. "Abortion Statistics: United States Data and Trends." Aug 13, 2019. https://nrlc.org/nrlnewstoday/2019/08/abortion-statistics-united-states-data-and-trends-2/.

BIBLIOGRAPHY

National University. "Women in Higher Education." https://www.nu.edu/blog/women-in-higher-education/.

"New Study Links Abortion to Wide Range of Mental Health Disorders." Foundation for Christian Counseling, Dec 11, 2008. https://www.ffcc4u.com/2024/06/27/new-study-links-abortion-to-wide-range-of-mental-health-disorders/.

Nouwen, Henri. *Adam: God's Beloved*. Maryknoll, NY: Orbis, 1997.

Phares, Ross. *Bible in Pocket, Gun in Hand: The Story of Frontier Religion*. Lincoln, NE: Bison Books, 1971.

Pocket Oxford American Dictionary. 2nd ed. New York: Oxford University Press, 2008.

"Post Abortion Syndrome: Summary, Symptoms, Frequency." http://www.religioustolerance.org/abo_pot.html.

Rosen, Christine. *The Extinction of Experience: Being Human in a Disembodied World*. New York: Norton, 2024.

Ruiz, John. *Living with Post Traumatic Stress Disorder*. Bloomington, IN: Authorhouse, 2004.

Ruth, Elizabeth. *Daily Readings with St. John of the Cross*. Springfield, IL: Templegate, 1986.

Savodnik, Peter. "How Intellectuals Found God." The Free Press, Dec 28, 2024. https://www.thefp.com/p/how-intellectuals-found-god-ayaan-hirsi-ali-peter-thiel-jordan-peterson.

Schnase, Robert. *Five Practices of Fruitful Congregations*. Nashville: Abingdon, 2007.

Senior, Donald. *The Passion of Jesus in the Gospel of John*. Collegeville, MN: Liturgical, 1991.

Sprague, C. Joseph. *Affirmations of a Dissenter*. Nashville: Abingdon, 2002.

Stallsworth, Paul T. "The United Methodist Church Leaves the Religious Coalition for Reproductive Choice."

Strobel, Lee. *The Case for Christ: A Journalist's Personal Investigation of the Evidence for Jesus*. Grand Rapids: Zondervan, 1998.

Thompson, Marianne Meye. "The Gospel of John and Early Trinitarian Thought: The Unity of God in John, Irenaeus and Tertullian." *Journal of Early Christian History* 4 (2014) 154–66.

Tutu, Desmond. *God Has a Dream: A Vision of Hope for Our Time*. New York: Doubleday, 2004.

United Methodist Africa Forum. "Open Letter on General Conference Preparations." https://www.umcafricaforum.org/news/open-letter.

Warren, Rick. *The Purpose Driven Life: What on Earth Am I Here For?* Grand Rapids MI: Zondervan, 2002.

"We Affirm: Religious Organizations Support Reproductive Choice." www.rcrc.org.

Wilberforce, William. *Real Christianity*. Ventura, CA: Regal, 2006.

www.ingramcontent.com/pod-product-compliance
Lightning Source LLC
Chambersburg PA
CBHW050833160426
43192CB00010B/2007